Coping with Loss

praying your way to acceptance

Carol Luebering

ST. ANTHONY MESSENGER PRESS
Cincinnati, Ohio

Scripture passages, unless otherwise noted, have been taken from *New Revised Standard Version Bible,* copyright ©1989 by the Division of Christian Education of the National Council of the Churches of Christ in the U.S.A., and used by permission. All rights reserved.

Cover and book design by Mark Sullivan
Cover image © istockphoto.com/Doreen Salcher

LIBRARY OF CONGRESS CATALOGING-IN-PUBLICATION DATA
Luebering, Carol.
Coping with loss : praying your way to acceptance / Carol Luebering.
p. cm.
ISBN 978-0-86716-847-1 (pbk. : alk. paper) 1. Bereavement—Religious aspects—
Catholic Church. 2. Prayer—Catholic Church. 3. Consolation. I. Title.
BX2373.B47L84 2008
248.8'6—dc22

2008046376

ISBN 978-0-86716-847-1

Published by St. Anthony Messenger Press
28 W. Liberty St.
Cincinnati, OH 45202
www.SAMPBooks.org

Printed in the United States of America.

Printed on acid-free paper.

09 10 11 12 13 5 4 3 2 1

contents

preface

When it comes to prayer, I can't pretend to be an expert. I am, like most people, one of those who pray—and sometimes struggle mightily. Neither am I an expert on grief, though I have known it more intimately than I ever wished to. And I have been involved in ministry to grieving people for many a year as a friend, as part of parish efforts and through my writings. You will find my story and the stories I have gleaned from others in these pages.

Other people's stories will never be an exact match for your own, for the pain that follows the rupture of any relationship is as unique as the relationship and the people involved in it. Nevertheless, another's story of struggling with loss may be woven of enough common threads to be helpful to you.

So the only credentials I can offer are those gained in the school of experience. And, as someone once observed, experience is not a good teacher at all because a good teacher would never give the test before the lesson. I flunked my first test in grieving: I gave up on God. Happily, God did not give up on me but filled my life with wonderful people who helped me get back in touch.

My prayer for you is that I can help you *keep* in touch with God all through the long and stormy season of grief. I hope this book will help you rediscover the ways of praying that once came easily and perhaps suggest some unfamiliar efforts, some of which may not sound to you like praying at all until you try them.

And my own prayers will be with you as you struggle through this long, hard season.

introduction

THE SEASON OF GRIEF

We have watched the seasons turn all our lives. The arrival of spring may make us catch our breath with delight, but it holds no more surprise than the arrival of any other season. Unless we have just moved from one climate to another—from New England to the Sun Belt, say—we know exactly what to expect from each turn of the calendar. The seasons of the church year are just as familiar. We know that Advent marks a period of waiting, that Lent invites us to reflection and repentance and that we will sing alleluias all through Eastertide.

The seasons of life are longer and a bit less predictable, but at least they usually unfold slowly. We gradually grow accustomed to each of them as we move from childhood to adulthood and on to middle age and the so-called golden years. Some of these seasons—adolescence for one—can, of course, be counted on to bring some stormy weather, but all of them clearly have an end in sight.

One season comes upon us without warning: the season of grief. It begins with a violent storm, an enormous loss. Any loss—job, home, financial security—can mark its beginning, but the death of a loved one is perhaps the most difficult to cope with. This book is directed especially to those who have buried someone dear. However, I recognize that many of the feelings, hurts and pains one experiences from the loss of a loved one to death are similar to those who have been divorced, laid off from work or lost their home or former way of life because of catastrophic circumstances, weather or finances.

Grief is a surprisingly long season, seeming endless at times. At first we think if we can just make it through the initial shock, we'll be OK. We quickly discover that the weather is taking a turn for the worse. We are lashed by constantly recurring extremes: the dead calm of disbelief that psychologists call denial, floods of tears, storms of rage, the oppressive atmosphere of depression. And just as nature's storms can reshape a coastline or change the course of a river, so can significant loss alter the landscape of our lives beyond recognition.

Even our relationship with God can shift on its foundation, making prayer a difficult exercise. Like the exiled Hebrews living as slaves in Babylon, we protest that we cannot sing the Lord's praises in an alien land (see Psalm 137:1–4). We can no longer carry on our conversation with God in the ways to which we are accustomed. Prayers that have grown familiar over the years suddenly taste like dust in our mouths.

You may have heard people talk about the "stages" of grief. But these periods of intense emotional impact do not follow each other in tidy progression; they have no predictable season like hurricanes or droughts do. Every time you think you have one season behind you, you suddenly find yourself back in it. They *can* be defined by certain characteristics just as nature's storms can.

This book is divided into sections that offer suggestions for prayer in different types of storms: denial, pain, anger, guilt and depression, all of which are defined below. The final section looks ahead in prayer to the end of grief's season, to the acceptance that often feels so impossibly far away.

The Storms of Grief

Denial: Loss has a way of catching us off guard, and our first response is denial. That doesn't mean that we say that this awful thing has not happened. More often we simply can't grasp the fact. Denial usually begins as disbelief.

Even when a loss has long been expected—even awaited as a merciful release from worry or suffering—we are surprised when it comes. We plan a funeral, but we stumble through it like robots, accepting the condolences of friends and shedding tears without beginning to comprehend that this loss is permanent. We keep expecting to find a lost loved one at home or in some other familiar place—not just in the first few days, but for a surprisingly long time. Many times we find ourselves forgetting the painful fact. We hear ourselves saying that he will really like something or thinking of what we must remember to tell her.

The unthinkable reality will eventually sink in, although we sometimes try to avoid it because it is very painful. In the meantime we struggle to pray without knowing what it is we need to ask for. At this point we need to pray for the courage to try coming to terms with the truth.

Pain: Loss hurts. It hurts all the time. It monopolizes your attention. The pain takes many forms. It may be as sharp as a knife, cutting your soul in two. It may be a dull ache that never quite goes away. It rolls over you in unexpected waves. You may find yourself bursting into tears without warning—or you may wish you could cry and wash the hurt out.

People who have had a limb amputated speak of "ghost pains"—feeling an ache in the calf of a leg that is no longer there. When we lose someone we love, we lose a piece of ourselves, and the loss leaves a gaping, throbbing wound. We define ourselves in large part by our relationships: I am spouse, son or daughter, parent, close friend. We have to learn not only to live without that special someone; we have to learn all over again who we are. And, just as it took a long time when we first figured it out, it won't happen quickly this time. The prayers in this section turn to God's loving arms for comfort.

Anger: When anger boils within us, we are ashamed of it. We know it isn't "nice" to be angry; if we remember the seven deadly sins, we know that what we feel is among that number. And Jesus' words about forgiveness echo in our hearts.

Yet that despised emotion is a reflection of the One in whose image we are made, a sign that a passion for justice is woven into our inmost being. When something seems unfair, our first reaction is to bristle. That blessed passion has led millions of people to resist injustice over the ages.

It is therefore quite natural for that emotion to rear its head when we have suffered a great loss. We want to hold someone responsible for the pain we feel. We may blame the doctors, the driver of the other car, ourselves. We may even be horrified to find ourselves blaming the beloved dead for leaving us. Scariest of all, we may find our fury directed toward God.

It helps to remember that feelings are not something we invite into our hearts; they rise spontaneously. *Nurturing* the feeling is another matter. The best way to deal with anger is to talk it out with someone who listens with love and understanding. And that's exactly why we need to carry it with us into our prayer. This section offers prayers that deal with our anger. Many of them involve our bodies as well as our hearts, for when we are angry we want to do something physical.

Guilt: We turn our anger on ourselves as well. We feel guilty for every failure in our relationship with the beloved dead. Regrets haunt us: If only we had said this, done that, known better, been there. We even take blame for the loss itself. Surely we should have noticed the symptoms sooner, kept a loved one off the road a little longer, picked up the clues of suicidal intent. Feelings of guilt walk hand in hand with grief. And the only way to resolve them is to seek forgiveness—not only from God, but also from your loved one. Because love is the only thing that is stronger than death, you can reach out in prayer with your apologies.

The prayers in this section suggest how to seek forgiveness where it is needed—and are designed to help you forgive yourself for your all-too-human failures.

Depression: Depression is the dreariest symptom of grief. Unlike sadness, it does not stab your heart with pain or fill you with a constant ache. Rather, it settles over you like a blanket of lead.

Your wheels just keep spinning. You run down the list of things you ought to do but can't bring yourself to make even the smallest beginning. Everything—even getting out of bed in the morning—seems to take too much effort, more energy than you can muster. You just want to put your head down and sleep, but you toss and turn—or, if sleep does come, you waken just as tired as you were when you closed your eyes. Hope shrivels and dies under the pall of your gloom.

Friends and family begin to tell you to snap out of it and get on with your life, but you cannot imagine what promise your life may yet hold. In time people begin to avoid your company. Even God seems distant and prayer an impossible effort. You wish you were the one who died and may even think of suicide.

Your idea of a perfect day is to pull the covers over your head and stay in bed. A better choice is to hide out in the vastness of God just as an unhappy child clings to a parent for comfort. The prayers in this section demand of you as little effort as possible.

Acceptance: The goal, the long-sought gift of peace, is accept-ance. It does not arise suddenly, like the sun bursting through the rain clouds. Rather, we reach it slowly and gradually. We begin to realize that the unthinkable loss has truly occurred. Sorrow becomes a less constant ache and the clouds of depres-sion lift. Anger dissipates and the burden of guilt lightens.

Acceptance is one of the gifts with which God loves to shower us. And so the final section of prayers in this book explores ways to ask for this gift. Turn to it often.

How to Use This Book

Using the definitions above, determine which storm is currently buffeting you. Then take a look at the table of contents until you find a title that seems to speak to what you are feeling. If the suggestions for prayer you find there are not comfortable to you, browse a bit further until you find something that fits. Always remember that it isn't the form of the prayer that mat-ters, but how well it helps you turn to God.

part one

PRAYING

YOUR

WAY

THROUGH

DENIAL

When You Can't Empty the Closet

A few weeks after Juanita's son died, her sister Maria offered to help her collect his things and get them to someone who could use them. Juanita told her, "Maria, I'm just not ready to do that yet. It would be like burying him all over again."

"But Juanita," Maria said, "he isn't going to need them again." Juanita realized that Maria had named the reason for her hesitation. She didn't want to move her son's things out, she admitted, because she thought—not consciously, of course—that if she kept them he'd come back for them. "He isn't going to need them ever again, is he?" Juanita said, and the two women fell into each other's arms and cried.

On the first Easter morning, Mary Magdalene stood weeping outside Jesus' empty tomb because she did not know where his body had been taken. This is how John tells the story:

> ...[S]he turned round and saw Jesus standing there, but she did not know that it was Jesus. Jesus said to her, "Woman, why are you weeping? For whom are you looking?" Supposing him to be the gardener, she said to him, "Sir, if you have carried him away, tell me where you have laid him, and I will take him away." Jesus said to her, "Mary!" She turned and said to him in Hebrew, "Rabbouni!" (which means Teacher). Jesus said to her, "Do not hold on to me...." (John 20:14–17)

Like Jesus, the person you love has moved on to a new and lasting life and no longer needs earthly possessions. Certainly you will always want to keep those possessions which have special meaning for you, but that hardly includes every sock in the drawer or garment in the closet. They won't help you to hold on to the one you have lost. Pray for the strength to give some things—even a few at a time—to someone who has need of them. Ask someone else to take them out of the house for you, if that is easier. Keep a favorite sweater to wrap yourself in, perhaps. Most of all pray for the faith to believe that the one you love is still and will always be part of you deep inside your heart.

. . . . .

When Nobody Wants to Hear the Story Again

Catherine's last months were a nightmare. Her illness kept her in constant pain in spite of the best efforts of hospice care. "Why doesn't God just take me?" she kept asking her husband. But Carl had no answer for her. Much as he hated the thought of losing her, he was more than ready to let her go.

After her death, Carl kept reliving the agony of watching her suffer. Over and over again he told everyone all the details until no one would listen anymore. "You have to put that behind you," they'd tell him. But soon he'd start all over again.

You may find yourself doing the same thing: replaying the details of your loss until no one wants to hear it again. You can't explain to others what you probably don't even realize yourself: that you have to keep repeating it until you believe it yourself.

Accept your need to replay your loss. In your prayer, join it to someone else's suffering. Get out your rosary and pray the Sorrowful Mysteries.

Someone once likened a person praying the rosary to an unhappy toddler sitting on a mother's lap, sobbing "Mommy, Mommy!" over and over again. Picture yourself in that position. Reflect on the mysteries. How do you think Mary felt watching her son suffer and die? How did Jesus feel when he agonized in the garden? When he felt the soldiers' whips tear into his skin? When he was crowned with thorns and mocked by his torturers? As he carried the heavy cross through the streets of Jerusalem? When he hung on the cross?

Meanwhile, standing near the cross of Jesus were his mother, and his mother's sister, Mary the wife of Clopas, and Mary Magdalene. When Jesus saw his mother and the disciple whom he loved standing beside her, he said to his mother, "Woman, here is your son." Then he said to the disciple, "Here is your mother." (John 19:25–27)

Retell your story of suffering and loss to Jesus and Mary, and know that they will listen as often as you need them to.

. . . . .

When You Feel Your Loved One's Presence

I had the privilege of taking Communion to Joe and Amy one Sunday a month when she was no longer up to going to church. I'd spend a leisurely time reflecting on the day's Scriptures with this deeply spiritual couple and listening to their endless supply of fascinating stories. At one time during his service in the Second World War, Joe was mistakenly reported as killed in action. "I didn't believe it," Amy told me, laying a hand over her heart. "I'd have known it *here*."

Amy's heart condition grew worse, but Joe didn't believe the doctors when they told him there was nothing more they could do for her. He couldn't even think of letting her go. The last time I visited them, Joe was insisting that she was going to be better soon, but something in her face told me she knew better. I reached for her hand and held it until I left. A few days later, Joe woke up in the morning and found her lying dead beside him.

They'd been married for fifty-five years. In her obituary Joe called her not only his wife but also his best friend. "She still seems to be here," Joe tells me now. "She visits me every now and then, and that's a joy."

Do I think he's out of his mind? Not at all! Neither are you, for the bond of love is the most indestructible thing in the world.

4

Continue to hold fast to the love you and your dear one shared. You believe that even death has no power to destroy it; strengthen your conviction by praying over these ancient words of wisdom:

> ...[T]he souls of the just are in the hands of God,
> and no torment will ever touch them.
> In the eyes of the foolish they seemed to have died,
> and their departure was thought to be a disaster,
> and their going from us to be their destruction,
> but they are at peace....
> [T]heir hope is full of immortality. (Song of Solomon 3:2–3, 4b)

. . . . .

When You Keep Forgetting

"He isn't there." In the months after her husband died, I heard my sister Pat say that many times. When a friend asked her where his grave was, Pat gave her directions and added, "But he isn't there." When I saw her wearing his sweater and asked if that made him feel closer, I got the same reply.

Recently she cleaned out the bathroom drawer where he kept his medicines, his hearing aid batteries and an assortment of other small things to make room for something else. She found a bottle of his aftershave lotion. "Don't open that," she told herself, but off came the lid anyway. She took a sniff—and found that it smelled like alcohol. "See, I told you he wasn't there," she chided herself.

Pat has always carried on lively conversations with herself. She assures me that is perfectly normal; it signals a problem only when you catch yourself asking, "What did you say?" But this conversation has a different ring from, "Now where did I put that?" or "What should I plan for dinner tomorrow?" I think she repeats it to help herself believe the truth she is struggling to accept. It has become her mantra.

In Eastern religions, a mantra is a mystic word or sound that is repeated in meditation. In a sense, it is similar to the old Catholic habit of repeating a short prayer such as a "Lord, have mercy" or "Jesus is Lord!" Contemplatives often focus on a single word to still their minds and center themselves in God's presence.

Try using a mantra in your prayer. Keep it short and simple, perhaps "not there" or simply your loved one's name. Acknowledge the emptiness you feel within. Be very still and slowly let God's loving presence fill you.

Finish your prayer by asking for the strength to believe that the person you loved really isn't physically present anymore. Borrow these ancient words of complaint, if you like, changing the pronouns if you need to:

> Upon my bed at night
>   I sought him whom my soul loves;
> I sought him, but found him not;
>   I called him, but he gave no answer.
> "I will rise now and go about the city,
>   in the streets and in the squares;
> I will seek him whom my soul loves."
>   I sought him, but found him not. (Song of Solomon 3:1–2)

. . . . .

When You Still Can't Believe It

Several months ago, Karen's daughter Sue suffered a massive head injury in an automobile accident. "I know she is dead," Karen says. "I kissed her good-bye just before the respirator was shut off. Her name is already on the grave marker. It's all very

6

clear in my head—but my heart still can't believe it. "Just the other day I caught a glimpse of a girl about Sue's age walking half a block ahead of me. Something about the way she tossed her long hair over her shoulder, the way she strode down the street—surely that was my daughter! I turned and followed her for several blocks. When she rounded a corner and I could see her profile, I had to admit it wasn't Sue. I knew all along it wasn't my daughter, of course—at least in my head. Why can't my heart remember as clearly as my head does?"

There is more than one way to remember. Early on, a human infant develops muscle memory—how to turn toward the sound of a voice, how to smile in response, how to reach toward something. And muscle memory is the longest lasting. Unless you suffer brain damage, you will always know how to move in order to accomplish a certain purpose.

What the mind learns is straightforward and logical: Two plus two is four; my book is on the table in the other room. Facts can, of course, slip from the mind for a moment or get lost forever. How often have you hunted for the thing that was right in your hand just a minute ago or groped for someone's name? Do you remember what the capital of Venezuela is or how to solve a quadratic equation? What a healthy mind has lost can be relearned with much less than the original effort.

The heart can be stubbornly resistant to learning, especially when that which must be learned is painful. It cannot be force-fed knowledge but must be allowed the time it needs to absorb an awful reality. Reflect on these ancient words:

For everything there is a season, and a time for every matter under heaven:

...

a time to weep and a time to laugh;
    a time to mourn, and a time to dance...(Ecclesiastes 3:1, 4)

7

In your prayer, recall some of the most important changes of season that have occurred in your life. When was your heart light enough for laughing and dancing? When was it heavy with tears and sorrow? Ask God to help you make it through this difficult time, to bring your heart to the certain knowledge of your loss so that you can begin to let the wound heal.

. . . . .

When You Still Can't Face the Reality

"Ever since their mother died," Hank says, "my kids have been on my back to get things done. Have I ordered the grave marker yet? How about cleaning out her closet? Shouldn't I hire someone to take care of cleaning the house? Maybe I should think about moving to a retirement home where someone else would do the cooking. I keep telling them I'll get to all that in good time.

"What I haven't been able to explain to them is that this is definitely *not* a good time. Everywhere I turn I slam into some reminder that she is gone. I don't need to work at remembering what I need to do. I just want to stop thinking about her death.

"Finally my oldest daughter caught on, but she wasn't very sympathetic. 'Oh Dad,' she told me, 'you sound just like Scarlett O'Hara. When is this *tomorrow* when you're going to start thinking about it?' I have no idea. I just know I'm not ready!"

It's all right not to feel ready. The pain of knowing we have lost someone important is not something anyone is eager to face; naturally we want to protect ourselves from it as long as possible. But, as Hank discovered, reminders are everywhere you turn.

The friends of Jesus were in much the same state after his death. They huddled together in the Upper Room, afraid that the people who conspired against him would come after them next. They had no idea how they were going to carry on without the person in whom they had placed all their faith.

Reflect on the words that Jesus spoke to them in that same room on the night before he died: "I still have many things to say to you, but you cannot bear them now. When the Spirit of truth comes, he will guide you into all the truth..." (John 16:12-13). And the Spirit did indeed! On Pentecost they began to carry on with life so boldly that we believe in their Lord centuries later.

In your prayer, turn to the empowering Spirit. Remember how that Spirit shook like a strong wind the room where the frightened apostles gathered in Acts 2:1-4. Read how Jesus breathed that Spirit gently into his friends at the end in John 20:19-22. Give thanks that the same Spirit was given to you in baptism and confirmation.

Take a deep breath and relax. Listen to your beating heart, and know that the life the Spirit gives flows throughout your body. Pray for an increase of some of the gifts the Spirit has already given: strength and courage, wisdom and understanding. And ask that consoling Spirit to help you begin absorbing the unthinkable reality of your loss.

.   .   .   .   .

When You Want to Look Somewhere Else

After my dad retired, he and my mother moved to the Sun Belt. They quickly made good friends; they loved it there. But when they had been there just over a year, my dad died.

A few months later, Mother decided to go back to their hometown in the Midwest to take a look at a retirement home where an old friend was living. My sister and I had a fit. "Remember

how you hated the winters," we told her, but off she went—
while we held our breath.

She called us when she got back to Arizona. "I have decided
to stay where I am," she told us. "The retirement home was nice
enough, but there are plenty of nice ones here. It isn't that the
winters back home scared me off. I realized when I got back to
Kansas that I kind of thought I'd find your dad there—where we
had spent so many years together. But he wasn't there."

My mother didn't consciously know what she was looking for
when she went back to Kansas. Perhaps you have a keener
sense of what you are seeking. But wherever you hunt for the
person you loved, he or she is not to be found anywhere on this
earth. Your head knows this, but your heart is a slow learner. Be
patient with yourself; allow yourself plenty of time to let the
painful reality sink in.

In the meantime, reflect on these words from an ancient
love song:

Upon my bed at night
    I sought him whom my soul loves;
I sought him, but found him not;
    I called him, but he gave no answer.
"I will rise now and go about the city,
    in the streets and in the squares;
I will seek him whom my soul loves."
    I sought him, but found him not. (Song of Solomon 3:1–2)

Since everything in Scripture points to God, you can read these
lines as an expression of God's longing for the beloved—and
that beloved is you, me and all the people on earth.

In your prayer, turn to the God whose heart also aches with
longing. Ask for support in your search and the courage to realize that you seek in vain. Relax in the loving divine arms that
ache to hold you.

part two

PRAYING

YOUR

WAY

THROUGH

PAIN

When a Birthday Is Coming

"When our oldest son was small," Bill says, "Elaine's mother gave him a copy of Dr. Seuss's *Happy Birthday to You!* There is one passage in it that quickly became Elaine's favorite. In this delightful bit of wacky verse, the author notes that you wouldn't be who you are if you hadn't been born and explores a list of things that you might be instead. The worst possibility of all is that you might be a 'wasn't, who has no fun at all.' Elaine was big on birthdays—celebrations of someone's existence, as she called them. She read that passage out loud. She'd even call the kids long after they were grown and gone just to recite it. Now her birthday is coming up, and all I can think of is that Elaine is now 'a wasn't.' Where she used to be is just a throbbing wound in my heart."

Believers, of course, don't think that someone who has died has really ceased to exist. Nevertheless, our beloved dead are painfully absent from our world and our lives. Like Bill, you have only a throbbing ache where someone dear used to be. The one you love has, in a sense, become "a wasn't" for you. He or she lives in God's presence—but so do you.

In your prayer, put yourself in God's presence and reflect on these words:

> But the souls of the righteous are in the hand of God,
> and no torment will ever touch them.
> In the eyes of the foolish they seem to have died,
> and their departure was thought to be a disaster,
> and their going from us to be their destruction;
> but they are at peace. (Wisdom of Solomon 3:1–3)

Recall that you are also in God's hands, and you are held tenderly by those hands all through your life. Picture yourself resting there, and picture the one you have loved and lost there beside you. Ask God to give you a sense of always being close to that person with whom God holds you.

. . . . .

When the Calendar Reminds You

"The calendar was my worst enemy, especially throughout the first year," Carla says. "Every time I looked at it, I hit a reminder of all that I have lost. It was not just the big dates that put a knife in my heart. I expected to dread them: the holidays, Lou's birthday, important anniversaries. But I didn't anticipate being hit below the belt by so many other ordinary days. Lou died, for instance, on a Tuesday, the fifth of the month. So every Tuesday and the fifth day of any month became painful reminders. Add to that the day we learned of the diagnosis, the point where we realized it was terminal, the date we started to check out hospice care, the last time the kids were here to say their good-byes —the list seemed endless."

We think of time as something concrete and measurable. That's true in the sense of how long it takes the Earth to spin on its axis or to complete its annual journey around the sun. But our emotions measure time in quite a different way. Think of the way it flies when you are having a wonderful time and how it drags when you are waiting impatiently for something or someone. Emotional responses also shape our reaction to particular days or dates. Probably no one ever said every week, "Thank God it's Monday!"

As Carla learned, great sorrow also sets certain times apart, especially in the first year. Their impact lessens the second time around and continues to ebb as the years go by.

It would be nice to avoid the calendar altogether, but that's just not possible in this world. Instead, take the day that is troubling you into your prayer with you. Reflect on the words of the psalmist:

This is the day that the LORD has made;
let us rejoice and be glad in it. (Psalm 118:24)

You have surely sung those words in every Easter season, for the glory of the Resurrection is Christianity's most precious memory. Remember, however, that what we celebrate at every Eucharist is not only the wonder of Easter but also the horror of Good Friday. The bread and wine we share when we "do this in memory of me" are the body broken and the blood poured out on our behalf.

Ask God to help you see even the hard days as a gift, an essential part of your healing. Give thanks for the infinite love that gave the only Son and ask that Son to touch your aching heart with his own wounded hands.

. . . . .

When Nobody Will Talk About Your Loved One

Sam and Susan's first baby Kevin was only eight months old when he died. He had enormous blue eyes, a winning smile and a fatal genetic defect. "He was the joy of our lives, even though we knew from the beginning that he wasn't ours to keep," says Susan. "Sam and I were devastated when we lost him. I don't know how we would have survived without the support of our families and our friends.

"But now something awful is happening. No one will talk about Kevin anymore. People just never mention his name, and they quickly change the subject if I start talking about him. They just act like he never existed at all—and I feel like I have lost him all over again."

Susan's family and friends don't mean to add to her pain. Rather, they see the tears well up in her eyes when Kevin's name comes up, and they change the subject in a well-intentioned but mistaken effort to spare her more pain. They just don't understand that her memories are the only part of her son she can hold on to.

If the people who love you refuse to talk about your dead loved one, do what Susan didn't think to do: Call them on it. Explain how you feel when you act as though that person had never existed. Tell them how much you need your memories, even though they may bring tears to your eyes.

And address your prayer to the One who has never forgotten a loved one. Reflect on these words the prophet Isaiah spoke in God's name to a people who felt they had been forgotten:

> But Zion said, "The LORD has forsaken me,
>   my Lord has forgotten me."
> Can a woman forget her nursing child,
>   or show no compassion for the child of her womb?
> Even these may forget,
>   yet I will never forget you.
> See, I have inscribed you on the palms of my hands... (Isaiah 49:14–16)

No one knows the importance of remembering better than the God who commanded the Jews to remember the rescue from slavery in Egypt with the Passover meal, the God whose only Son told his followers to break bread and bless wine in memory of him.

Cherish your memories of the one you loved in the presence of this God. And know that God has not forgotten either of you.

When No One Understands How You Feel

"I'm beginning to feel like I've been transported into a country whose language I can't speak," Hank complains. "Neither can I find a soul who understands a word of mine. Since Katie died, no one seems to have any sense of what I am going through. And if I try to explain how hard it is to go on without her, all I get are blank looks. My closest friends don't have a clue about why I don't want to join in the activities we used to enjoy as a couple. Being with other happily married people is just more than I can bear right now.

"What I'd give to find just one person who understands! I've tried support groups, but it only makes me feel worse to listen to other people's sad stories."

Support groups can certainly be a wonderful help. Sharing your grief with someone who is struggling with the same feelings at least gives you the sense that you really haven't lost your mind.

The one drawback is that support groups seldom include survivors because people tend to drop out when their grief is resolved and they really are ready to get on with their lives. Where can you find someone whose experience will help you to believe that you really will heal?

In baptism every believer acquires the largest support group known to humankind: the communion of saints. We are surrounded, says the letter to the Hebrews, by a "great cloud of witnesses" (see Hebrews 12:1). Its number certainly includes many who have known grief and who have worked through their sorrows with God's help. Turn to them in your prayer.

Some are quite famous. To name just a few: Thomas More buried his wife, Jane Colte, after only six years of a very happy marriage. Elizabeth Ann Seton watched her husband die slowly of tuberculosis; she took in her first pupils to support herself and her children after his death. Isidore, patron saint of his fellow farmers, had only one child, a son who did not live to adulthood. Kateri Tekakwitha lost both parents and a little brother in a smallpox epidemic that left her disfigured and nearly blind. Others have never attained canonization, but some of them may have touched your life with love. Consider the departed friends and family members who knew grief intimately. Ask these holy friends to pray for you, to stay close beside you as you make the long journey toward acceptance of your own loss.

. . . . .

When People Avoid You

When Karen's husband died suddenly, her friends came running when she broke the news. They brought hugs and prayers and casseroles. They were with her all through the visitation and the funeral. But as the weeks wore on, she heard less and less from them.

"I was the first widow in our circle," she says. "I suppose none of my friends has any idea how it really feels. And they certainly don't want to hear about it! I feel like I have a dreadful, contagious disease that everyone is afraid of catching. I'm sure that's not really the problem; they just don't understand that I *need* to cry and to talk about what I have lost. But I feel so alone!"

Like Karen, you may feel that your friends are avoiding you. However well you understand their confusion, it leaves you in pain. Borrow the words of the Psalmist to complain to God:

You have caused my companions to shun me;
    you have made me a thing of horror to them.
I am shut in so that I cannot escape;
    my eye grows dim through sorrow. (Psalm 88:8–9)

17

Remembering how little you knew about grief before your loss, hold your friends in your prayer, asking for the wisdom to realize that they are doing the best they can.

And seek someone who has known sorrow to pray with you and for you. Pray also for or with someone who does understand. Perhaps try a support group or ask the people who minister in your community to put you in touch with someone. Don't forget to ask the people you have known for help, the folks who are now with God themselves.

．．．．．

When You Can't Find Any Comfort

In her living room Sarah has a very old rocking chair made by her great-grandfather. The cutout flowers on its back are obviously handmade because they are uneven. Because it is put together with glued wooden pegs instead of nails, it creaks when it rocks. "I remember being rocked in it as a small child," Sarah says. "The sound it made as my grandma held me was like a lullaby. Her arms were wrapped around me, and I could hear the sound of her heartbeat. I felt wrapped in love.

"I'm not a small child anymore—far from it. But when the little girl in me feels the need for a little comfort I sit down in Granny's old chair and rock—sometimes for hours. The creak-creak-creak of that old chair puts me right back in her arms, and I soak up the love and comfort she gave me decades ago."

Consider what God said to Israel through his prophet many centuries ago:

When Israel was a child, I loved him,

. . .

I led them with cords of human kindness,
     with bands of love.
I was to them like those

who lift infants to their cheeks.

I bent down to them and fed them. (Hosea 11:1, 4)

Settle into your favorite comfortable spot—a rocker perhaps, or an easy chair—and picture God holding you with all the tenderness of a parent with an infant or a grandparent with a tiny tot. Relax in the divine arms and remember someone who comforted you when you were little, assuring you that everything would be all right. Hear God's voice repeating the same words. Feel your loving Maker gently stroking your hair; feel the infinite love in the arms that hold you. Stay as long as you need to.

. . . . .

When People Won't Let You Cry

"If I had a nickel for every time someone has told me to stop crying," Ruth says, "I wouldn't know what to do with all that money. For that matter, I keep telling myself the same thing, but it doesn't help a bit. The tears just keep coming. Forget that nonsense about how crying makes you feel better. It just makes my nose stuffy and my eyes red, while the pain goes on and on and on! It makes me angry when people insist that I shouldn't cry. It would be a lot more helpful if they would just pass the tissues or put their arms around me and let their shoulders get soggy."

Another person's tears make us uncomfortable. And they should! Imagine what would happen to infants if no one paid attention to their cries. (The human race would have died out long ago!) And we know by instinct what to do with a crying baby: Open our arms and hold the child until the sobbing abates.

Our instincts don't serve us as well with weeping adults. Because we feel helpless, we try to stop the flood with words, and often our words are not chosen well. The God in whose image we are made knows better. Centuries ago, the prophet Isaiah described someone who was to come in God's name with these words:

> The spirit of the Lord GOD is upon me,
>   because the LORD has anointed me;
> he has sent me to bring good news to the oppressed,
>   to bind up the broken-hearted,
> ...
> to comfort all who mourn. (Isaiah 61:1, 2)

Christians have long identified that someone with Jesus, for we remember him as one who was always sensitive to human pain and sorrow. And we also remember that his earthly life ended on Calvary where, in the words of one liturgical prayer, he "opened his arms on the cross."

Make a crucifix the focus of your prayer. Hold one in your hand or picture it in your mind. See Jesus opening his arms to hold you as you weep. Lean into that loving embrace and cry as much as you need to.

. . . . .

When You Are Tired of Being in Pain

"I had shingles once," Jane recalls. "I had never known such pain. It was like being locked in a room with a whiny four-year-old; it demanded my constant attention. Even with the help of a doctor whose specialty was pain management, it lasted for months.

"This pain is worse. It doesn't afflict a single nerve like shingles did, but affects every aspect of my life. Neither is it constant. I go about my day and sometimes forget that my child is dead. Then I remember, and it is like a fresh stab in my heart all over again. It has been almost a year since Robby died. Will it ever stop hurting so much?"

If you break a leg, it will mend slowly, but you will notice that it is gradually getting better. It will give you a lot of pain at first, but one day you will say that it feels much better than it did. A broken heart doesn't heal in such a straightforward manner. Rather, it may feel like it was torn just yesterday even after months have gone by. It will, to be sure, heal enough that some-day you can live without constant pain. You still may feel a twinge or two many years later, but it will not be the crippling ache of the first year or two.

Nobody says it is easy to be patient when healing is slow. That's true of waiting for a broken bone to heal; it is even more difficult when you are waiting for your heart to heal.

Many centuries ago, a believer wrote about a man named Job who struggled to make sense of his suffering. His loss was great indeed. First everything he owned disappeared, and he man-aged to survive that. But then every one of his children died, and he was a broken man. He complained long and bitterly to God in words such as these:

My face is red with weeping,
  and deep darkness is on my eyelids,

. . .

My eye has grown dim from grief,
  and all my members are like a shadow,

. . .

My days are past, my plans are broken off,

. . .

where then is my hope? (Job 16:16; 17:7,11,15)

Follow Job's example and complain freely to God. Speak to him about your longing to be free of the pain you are feeling. Implore him for the courage to keep on putting one foot in front of the other all through the long season of your sorrow. Ask for the strength to face the loss of someone dear and to accept the pain as a necessary part of your healing, even when it seems endless.

. . . . .

When You Can't Cry

Sally learned not to cry when she was just a little girl. "My mother didn't believe in hitting children," she explains. "Emotional abuse was her weapon of choice. She would talk and talk and talk, belittling me and doing her best to reduce me to tears. The minute a tear appeared on my cheeks, she won. So I have always been so careful never to be seen crying that I've quite forgotten how to let the tears fall. I've buried a lot of people who were dear to me—my grandparents, my dad, a friend— and made it through their funerals without shedding a single tear. Joe's death was the most devastating loss I could possibly imagine. We were married for thirty-five years and his absence leaves a gaping hole in my heart. But my tears are a hard lump inside of me; they never make it to my eyes. How I wish I'd learned to cry!"

Even the most loving parents discourage tears. From earliest infancy they try to comfort us when we wail. As children grow older, they are told that big girls or boys (especially!) don't cry. The sound of human sobs distresses us—as well it should. For we are made in the image of a compassionate God, who formed us to respond to one another's pain. Unfortunately, we confuse stopping the tears with easing the sorrow.

If the inability to cry is an ache in your heart, try priming the pump. Rent the movie that once brought tears to your eyes or reread the book that made a lump in your throat and see if you can get the tears flowing.

Picture the water that flowed from Jesus' pierced side; think of the baptismal water that once flowed over your head. Reflect on this ancient promise and then pray for the gift of tears:

> I will open rivers on the bare heights,
> and fountains in the midst of the valleys;
> I will make the wilderness a pool of water,
> and the dry land springs of water. (Isaiah 41:18)

.   .   .   .   .

When You Don't Know Who You Are Anymore

"Today is Monday, my name is Sandra and the president is good old what's-his-face." That was what Sandra always joked when she had a "senior moment."

It hasn't seemed so funny since her twin sister died. "We were identical," she says. "All my life I could look in Karen's face and see myself. We were so much alike we could finish each other's sentences. I always knew myself as Karen's twin. I do still remember my name, but now I seem to have lost a great chunk of my sense of whom I am."

When someone dear to us dies, we lose a piece of ourselves. So largely do we define ourselves by our relationships that we scarcely know who we are when death shatters one. We have to learn all over again how to introduce ourselves. We struggle with saying that we are someone's widow or widower (horrid words!). We can no longer identify ourselves as this person's parent or sibling, as the son or daughter of a dead parent, as a dear friend of a person who has died.

We ache also to be known. Gone are the eyes in which we saw ourselves lovingly mirrored. Gone is someone with whom we could share many memories and secret jokes, a person to whom we could always safely reveal our inmost self.

Only the God who made us has always known each of us so well. Turn to your Maker in your prayer. Speak to God about your loneliness, your longing to know yourself and be known with love. Ask God to help you see who you are in the divine eyes, to glimpse especially the traits that make your Creator take delight in you. Close your prayer with the words of the psalmist:

O Lord, you have searched me and known me,
...
For it was you who formed my inward parts;
    you knit me together in my mother's womb.
I praise you, for I am fearfully and wonderfully made.
    Wonderful are your works;
that I know very well.
    My frame was not hidden from you,
when I was being made in secret,
    intricately woven in the depths of the earth.
Your eyes beheld my unformed substance.
In your book were written
    all the days that were formed for me,
        when none of them as yet existed. (Psalm 139:1, 13–16)

.   .   .   .   .

When You Miss Someone Very Much

Charlotte lost her husband just a few months ago. When I saw her at church a couple of weeks ago, I gave her a hug and asked how she was doing. "Putting one foot in front of the other," she replied.

"That's about all you can do, isn't it?" I asked her.

"Not quite," she told me. "He was nearly finished with a book, and now I'm editing it."

What a wonderful way to keep him close to her, I thought.

And then I had to smile because I once took on a similar project. I remembered the day my sister-in-law, Jane, and I spent on our knees in my living room. My mother-in-law had told me before she died that she had started quilts for two granddaughters. The blocks were finished and needed to be assembled. Could I do that?

Well yes, the blocks were finished and they were all together in one bag. All we had to do was figure out how to sort them into two quilt tops.

So there we were on the floor, trying to figure out what arrangement Mom had had in mind for all those squares while the dog helped by licking our faces with glee. Finally Jane sat back on her heels and laughed, "I bet Mom's up there enjoying all this!"

You may not have the skills to edit a book or finish a quilt. Nevertheless, everyone leaves some unfinished task behind. (I hope someone will finally get all those photos in my scrapbook!) Completing a pet project is something you can still do for the person for whom you are grieving. Think of it as a kind of memorial gift. If some learning is involved, it is also an opportunity. See if you can sense your loved one's pride in seeing the work finished or amusement in watching your ineptitude. Feel free to carry on a conversation with the person you miss so much. Express your puzzlement, your frustration or your pride—whatever the project brings to you.

And as you work on it remember that Jesus also left his work unfinished. Before he returned to the One who sent him, he commissioned his disciples to carry the Good News further and to baptize in his name. And reflect on these words from the Acts of the Apostles:

So when they had come together, they asked him, "Lord, is this the time when you will restore the kingdom to Israel?" He replied, "It is not for you to know the times or periods that the Father has set by his own authority. But you will receive power when the Holy Spirit has come upon you; and you will be my witnesses in Jerusalem, in all Judea and Samaria, and to the ends of the earth." When he had said this, as they were watching, he was lifted up, and a cloud took him out of their sight. While he was going and they were gazing up towards heaven, suddenly two men in white robes stood by them. They said, "Men of Galilee, why do you stand looking up towards heaven?" (Acts 1:6–11)

. . . . .

When You Can't Face the Holidays

"They start playing Christmas carols earlier every year," Belinda says. "This year I'm turning off my car radio right after Halloween. I don't even want to think about Christmas. Jerry and I had decades of Christmases together and I don't know how I'm going to get through this one without him.

"My sister and my brother are both insisting that I should come to be with their families. My kids all are offering to host a family gathering. But I just don't want any part of it. I just want to pull the covers over my head and wake up when it's over."

Every holiday comes wrapped in family traditions. Whether you always had a picnic on the Fourth of July or organized an Easter egg hunt or opened your presents on Christmas Eve and then went to midnight services, your plans always included certain people.

And now someone important to you will be missing from the gathering. How will you get through it? Face it, there is no way you can recreate past holiday joys this year. But any effort just to pretend the holiday isn't coming is also doomed to fail.

In your prayer, ask God to help you see that all the holidays were much less joyful in their beginnings. Thanksgiving was, after all, preceded by a period of near-starvation. The first Fourth of July brought on a long and bitter war that divided neighbor against neighbor and often seemed doomed to failure.

Reread this familiar story:

> In those days a decree went out from Emperor Augustus that all the world should be registered.... All went to their own towns to be registered. Joseph also went from the town of Nazareth in Galilee to Judea, to the city of David called Bethlehem, because he was descended from the house and family of David. He went to be registered with Mary, to whom he was engaged and who was expecting a child. While they were there, the time came for her to deliver her child. And she gave birth to her firstborn son and wrapped him in bands of cloth, and laid him in a manger, because there was no place for them in the inn. (Luke 2:1, 3–7)

Put yourself in Joseph's and Mary's sandals on that first Christmas. They were surely both still confused over the strange events that had befallen them before they set out. The long journey must have been especially difficult for a woman whose pregnancy was far along. They could find shelter only in a stable, where the young woman gives birth miles away from the relatives and neighbors who might have offered help back home. Like every other newborn human, the child wails with pain when the cold air invades his unaccustomed lungs.

Remembering their discomfort (to put it mildly!), give yourself permission to be short of happy feelings in any holiday season. And ask the God on whom that couple relied to strengthen your faith as they were strengthened so that you can deal with all that comes along.

part three

PRAYING

YOUR

WAY

THROUGH

ANGER

When You're Angry at God

Carl was simply furious when his son died after a long and painful illness. And he directed his anger toward the one person most of us hesitate to argue with: God. Carl struggled to squelch his anger, but that only made it burn more fiercely.

Finally one day, at the suggestion of the confessor to whom he had poured out his anger, he sought out an empty church. Looking around very carefully to make sure he was alone, Carl began to shout his feelings at God. He screamed that God was a big bully, a cruel being who tortured innocent children and broke their parents' hearts. He raved at God until he fully expected to be struck by lightning at any moment. Finally he stopped, worn out by the effort.

"I didn't hear a voice thundering from the sky," he says. "But in my heart I sensed that God was agreeing that my son's death was a terrible tragedy. I suddenly felt that God was raging and weeping with me."

In pouring out his anger to God, Carl was in good company. God's closest friends have a long history of arguing with their Maker. Take Jeremiah, for one. As a youngster, he never dreamed of being a prophet when he grew up. But God called him when he was still young enough to protest that he wasn't old enough to take on such a challenge.

And it was no easy task God had in mind for young Jeremiah. He was given the unpleasant task of warning his people that the Lord was just about fed up with their sinful ways. Again and again Jeremiah had to warn them that they were courting disaster—which, of course, did little for his popularity. He complained again and again when no punishment was forthcoming from the patient divine hand. Once, he used these words:

O LORD, you have enticed me,
  and I was enticed;

you have overpowered me,
  and you have prevailed.
I have become a laughing-stock all day long;
  everyone mocks me.
For whenever I speak, I must cry out,
  I must shout, "Violence and destruction!"
For the word of the LORD has become for me
  a reproach and derision all day long. (Jeremiah 20:7–8)

To get the full sense of Jeremiah's complaint, you need to know that the word here translated as *enticed* has sexual overtones. Jeremiah is accusing God of seducing him!

In your prayer, follow the prophet's example. Tell God exactly how badly you feel you have been used. Remember that no human quarrel has ever been resolved by silence. Only by bringing the dispute out into the open can people who love each other begin to work out their disagreements. Trust God to be no less loving a listener than the dearest person you have ever known.

. . . . .

When You're Angry at the Dead

"My brother Jim," Ann remembers, "was a high school football coach. At his funeral, a lot of young men told me what a difference Jim had made in their lives. Some remembered that he had given them a swift kick you-know-where when they needed it. Others spoke of his patient encouragement. All of them agreed that, as a coach, he never insisted that they had to win, only that they had to play as well as they could.

"He was like that as my big brother, too. But he killed himself! Tell me why such a great guy could do such a terrible thing to everyone who cared about him. I just can't get over being mad at him. I'd like to dig him up and shake him!"

Maybe you feel as Ann does—not necessarily because some-one you love committed suicide, but for any one of many other reasons. Pick one or state your own: He should have gone to the doctor sooner; she should have stopped smoking; he took one too many foolish risks; she left you alone and confused.

Remember that feeling angry at your loved one is not a new experience. The big difference is that you could express it and work it out when he or she was still alive. Try to do the same thing now. Speak your anger and the reasons for it, trusting that just hearing yourself say it will help you begin to work it through. Remember all the times your anger cooled, all the times you managed to forgive perhaps even a serious wrong and continue to love.

Pray in the words that Jesus himself taught: the Our Father, lingering over the request to be forgiven as we forgive. Remember that when Jesus taught his followers this prayer this was the one phrase to which he added a comment: "For if you forgive others their trespasses, your heavenly Father will also forgive you; but if you do not forgive others, neither will your Father forgive your trespasses" (Matthew 6:14). Ask for the grace to let go of your anger and hold fast to the love you remember.

· · · · ·

When You're Angry at Someone Who Is Responsible
"I lost everything in a flash," says Gary. "My wife, who was eight months pregnant, was killed instantly. They delivered our son by cesarean and tried to save him, but he didn't make it either. The only time I got to hold him was when I put him in the cas-ket beside his mother. And all because some irresponsible teenager reached for a ringing cell phone!

"I've tried to feel sorry for the kid. He was only sixteen, with a brand-new driver's license. The judge threw the book at him, and I guess his life is pretty much in shambles too. Still, if I could get my hands on him...."

Holding someone responsible for your loss—the person who caused the accident, the medical personnel who didn't give the right treatment soon enough—seems to help you to make sense of the death that has caused you so much pain. Unfortunately, it doesn't really work. Your loss would be just as incomprehensible if you had no one to hold at fault.

Neither does nursing your anger make you feel better, for it only adds a taste of bitterness to the cup that has been forced to your lips. Only finding the ability to forgive will bring you healing and freedom.

No one pretends that forgiving is easy. But it must always lay within the realm of possibility because Jesus insisted that it is something we must do.

Bring your pain to God like a small child would, sobbing as God folds loving arms around you. See the loving concern in God's face; feel the tender touch of the hands that shaped you in your mother's womb.

And then let the brother or sister who has hurt you so badly come into that loving presence with you. See how God looks at that person: with the same boundless love and gentle pity in which you are basking. Ask God to help you see that person's woundedness, that one's terrible need for the love that sustains us all. Reach out and hold the other's hand in God's presence.

Trying to see someone through God's eyes is the first step toward forgiveness and peace. Keep trying through the days ahead until you feel your heart begin to soften.

When You're Angry at Yourself

The anger you turn against yourself has a better name: guilt—and that's another chapter. Please see Part Four: Praying Your Way Through Guilt.

. . . . .

When You're Angry at the Situation

"I knew my attitude toward the world in general was pretty bad," Georgia admits. "But it was my three-year-old grandchild who really brought it home to me. She looked up at me with those enormous brown eyes and asked me, 'Grandma, why are you mad at me?' I scooped her up and assured her that I wasn't mad at her. But how do you explain to such a little tot that you're angry at the situation in which you find yourself? I miss my husband every minute of every day! Everything is harder, from getting up in the morning to opening a jar, from eating alone to figuring out what to do about the car. Anger is a sinful thing, I know. But I'm not nursing it. It's just there, ready to rear its ugly head at the slightest thing."

Without realizing it, Georgia put her finger on an important truth: Anger isn't necessarily sinful. It is first simply an emotion, and emotions are not something we can keep from feeling. It's only in what we do with the feelings that we exhibit the power of choice, and therefore the power to consciously sin. If, for example, we direct our angry feelings toward another person and inflict harm, that is sinful. We can find some other outlet for it.

Anger has a physical effect on us: It is nature's way of preparing us to fight for our lives. It provokes a rush of adrenaline, and the best way to burn that off is to do something physical. When I was an adolescent, I worked off my frequent hot tempers by going into the garage and bouncing a tennis ball off the walls.

Pounding on your bed with a whiffle bat is equally harmless and just as effective, as is a brisk walk or a fast ride on a stationary bicycle.

Jesus once worked out his anger in that way. Reflect on the event described in this Scripture passage:

> The Passover of the Jews was near, and Jesus went up to Jerusalem. In the temple he found people selling cattle, sheep, and doves, and the money-changers seated at their tables. Making a whip of cords, he drove all of them out of the temple, both the sheep and the cattle. He also poured out the coins of the money-changers and overturned their tables. (John 2:13–15)

Hanging on my refrigerator is a little filler piece I clipped from somewhere. I keep it to remind me of this scene. It reads: "When someone asks you what Jesus would do, at least one correct answer is 'knock over some tables.'"

As you do whatever physical thing you find helps dispel your anger, remind the Lord of his mighty tantrum. Remember that he didn't use the whip on any person; he just shooed the animals out of the temple with it. Ask for the grace to use your anger in ways that are not hurtful, and trust that, like any other emotional storm, it will pass in time.

. . . . .

When You're Angry Because Everyone Else Seems Happy

"No, I'm not going to the parish picnic this year," Amanda told her friend Kerry. "I just can't stand to be with all those families having such a good time together when one of my children is lying in the cemetery. I know it's a terrible way to feel, but happy families make me so angry!"

"I don't think it's terrible at all," Kerry replied gently. "You're angry about your loss, not mad at other people for being happy."

"Oh, thank you for understanding," Amanda responded. "You have always been such a good friend to me! What would I do without you?"

"Hold on," Kerry added. "I'm not saying you're right! People don't usually wear their broken hearts on their sleeve. You have no way of knowing who lost a child before you ever knew them or whose marriage is on the verge of collapse or whose kid is hopelessly addicted to drugs. Sooner or later everyone knows some terrible pain; it's part of being human. Why don't you just look at the happy families and wonder how they manage so much joy with God-knows-what tragedy in their history?"

Kerry is not only a good friend; she is also a wise one. It's a rare human being indeed who never suffers. In his suffering, the biblical Job complained to God about the human situation in these words:

A mortal, born of woman, few of days and full of trouble,
  comes up like a flower and withers,
    flees like a shadow and does not last.
Do you fix your eyes on such a one? (Job 14:1–3)

The answer faith has held since the days of Moses is that God does indeed notice human suffering. Christian belief holds that God's only Son took on human flesh and knew pain and loss himself—and further, insisted that those who would follow him must also tend to the suffering.

In your prayer, place your own sorrow in his gentle hands. And carry with you into the presence of the Lord anyone you know who is also in pain of some sort. Ask him to help all of you to trust that one day you will leave today's sorrow behind and learn to laugh again.

When You're Angry Because Your Loss Seems Unfair
Sandy died a few months before his and his wife's forty-seventh wedding anniversary. When that date rolled around, Lydia was, not surprisingly, terribly sad. "We always looked forward to our golden anniversary celebration," she told her son. "We had even started thinking about just how we would celebrate it."

Trying to console her, Jay reminded her, "But you and Dad had such a good marriage. I bet you packed more love and joy into the years you had together than some folks manage in a lot more time."

"That's true," his mother agreed. "But that's exactly what makes it so hard. We know a lot of couples who have celebrated their golden anniversaries. You'd be surprised how many of them were people who had fought for years, even folks who were sometimes unfaithful to each other. It just doesn't seem fair that Dad and I couldn't have fifty years together when those people did!"

It doesn't help to say that life isn't fair, does it? Yet we all know that it isn't. Nevertheless, believers have long insisted that it *should* be. For countless centuries, there's been a misconception that living in accordance with God's will automatically ensures health, wealth and happiness.

So persistent has this belief been that one ancient biblical author wrote a book to challenge it. His protagonist is a man called Job, a just and God-fearing man who owned many flocks of sheep and herds of camels. He employed many servants and was the proud father of seven sons and three daughters.

Then, all in the course of one horrible day, he lost everything he owned and all his children. As if that weren't enough, his body erupted in boils.

The friends who came to comfort him in his affliction were sure that Job must have done something to displease God. Over and over they insisted that he must repent of his sins and over and over Job protested his innocence. He even wanted to put God on trial for treating him so unfairly.

Reflect on the words the inspired author puts in Job's mouth:

Today also my complaint is bitter;
  [God's] hand is heavy despite my groaning.
O, that I knew where I might find him,
  that I might come even to his dwelling!
I would lay my case before him,
  and fill my mouth with arguments.
I would learn what he would answer me,
  and understand what he would say to me.
Would he contend with me in the greatness of his power?
  No; but he would give heed to me. (Job 23:2–6)

If Job's words reflect your own feelings, know that God did indeed answer Job. Recalling the divine feats of creation, God kept asking Job, "And where were you when I did this?" In other words, God's answer was to ask Job if he could run the world any better, and Job had to back down.

In your prayer, remember how many innocent people suffer. Hear the cries of children in famine-stricken lands. Pity the refugees who flee the bombs and guns of war-torn lands. Weep with the parents whose children have fallen victim to violence —or whose children have become violent themselves. Whisper a prayer for people struck down by cruel diseases.

And know that these are the children your God holds most dear, the ones whose cries always reach the divine heart. Let yourself bask in the love that makes God's heart ache for you.

part four

PRAYING

YOUR

WAY

THROUGH

GUILT

When You Are Ashamed of Your Feelings

Jodie went to her pastor for counseling. "I used to think of myself as a really nice person," Jodie told him. "But when Al died, I turned into a monster. If a friend mentions an upcoming wedding anniversary, my eyes turn a brilliant green with jealousy. If someone wants a bit of sympathy for some crisis, all I can think is that I have a better right to complain. I'm angry, utterly downbeat, perfectly horrid to be with, I'm sure. And I feel awful about the way I feel. I am so ashamed!"

"But you're only talking about what you *feel*," the wise counselor replied. "Grief brings a lot of unpleasant feelings. So tell me what you *do* when they hit. Do you rage at the friend who is looking forward to an anniversary or refuse to listen to the person who is struggling with a crisis?"

Jodie looked shocked. "Of course not!" she replied.

"Feelings have no moral value in and of themselves," her pastor explained. "They just come without being chosen. It is, after all, the choices we make that are either good or bad. And it sounds like you are still making good choices."

"Then why do I feel so guilty?" Jodie asked.

"There is a world of difference between *feeling* guilty and *being* guilty," her adviser gently replied. People sometimes do horrendous things without feeling a twinge of guilt. Don't you wonder, for example, if Hitler ever felt a pang of regret over the fate of millions of Jews?"

If, like Jodie, you are ashamed of your feelings, take her pastor's advice to heart. Those feelings are likely to be with you for awhile, for unwelcome emotions are a normal part of the grieving process. You can't make them go away, so you might as well try to make peace with these uninvited guests.

Reflect on this passage from the Gospels:

Jesus went throughout Galilee, teaching in their synagogues and proclaiming the good news of the kingdom and curing every disease and every sickness among the people. So his fame spread throughout all Syria, and they brought to him all the sick, those who were afflicted with various diseases and pains, demoniacs, epileptics, and paralytics, and he cured them. (Matthew 4:23–24)

Invite your feelings into your prayer with you. Imagine them as persons with crippling conditions. Take them to Jesus and ask him to use his healing touch. Tell him your anger needs its bitterness softened, your sorrow is too heavy and needs to lose some weight. Ask him to lay his healing hands on your head and bring you the courage to accept whatever is going on inside you.

. . . . .

When You Feel Guilty For Being Happy

"My little grandson laughed out loud for the first time today when I blew on his tummy," Jody told her friend Sal. "I let out such a whoop of delight that I scared him into crying. And the thought crossed my mind that he had a better grasp of the situation than I did. I should have been crying, not laughing. This baby is such a joy to me, but I feel guilty taking such delight in him when his grandpa never even got to see him or hold him. Max was so thrilled when we learned this baby was on the way. He was always so good with little tots! He would have made a wonderful grandpa."

"You know," Sal mused, "when I was just a kid in grade school, one of my classmates lost his mother to cancer. We were talking about it in religion class—you now, asking how God could do such a thing to Bobby. Then our teacher asked a question no one could answer: 'How do you know that Bobby's mother can't take care of him from heaven as well as—maybe even better than—she could on earth?' Maybe Max is sitting up there in heaven admiring his grandson and thanking God that the little guy is giving you so much joy. Do you really think Max would want to see you crying all the time?"

Sal is right on the money! The person you have loved and lost would not begrudge you the most fleeting moment of happiness. Neither would he or she want to see you in pain, for none of us want to see someone we love suffer.

Neither does the God who made us and holds us constantly in infinite love. That God made us for joy—indeed, for everlasting bliss.

Read and reflect on what Jesus said to his friends as he prepared to go to his death:

When a woman is in labor, she has pain, because her hour has come. But when her child is born, she no longer remembers the anguish because of the joy of having brought a human being into the world. So you have pain now; but I will see you again, and your hearts will rejoice, and no one will take your joy from you. (John 16:21–22)

Remember how the apostles huddled together in fear and sorrow after Jesus' death and how they rejoiced when he returned to them—only to watch him disappear into heaven forty days later. Pray to your favorite among their number, asking that great saint to strengthen your faith that the moments of happiness you know now will lengthen and grow stronger—and that it is perfectly OK to feel happy even as you grieve.

. . . . .

When You Hold Yourself Responsible

Twelve-year-old Clare died instantly when she was struck by a car. The intersection was a busy one, but she was in the crosswalk and proceeding with the walk light when an inexperienced driver failed to hit the brake and flew through the red light.

At the funeral, her mother, Jill, was totally distraught. "She wouldn't have been there," her mother sobbed to anyone who would listen, "if I hadn't sent her to the store for something I forgot to buy. I sacrificed my daughter for a couple of onions, and I'll never forgive myself!"

And she didn't. Months later, Jill was still talking about the delightful child she had given up for those onions no matter how many friends challenged her logic. "Of course I didn't intend for her to die," she'd counter. "But the fact remains that she did—and all because I didn't pay attention to what I was doing when I went to the supermarket that week."

Obviously, Jill did not intentionally send her daughter to her death—nor would she have if she could have foreseen what would happen. None of us has 20/20 foresight. We can only do the best we can with the knowledge we have at the moment.

And that's surely exactly what Jill did—and maybe you are blaming yourself for not having done something more than that.

God can presumably see what is going to happen. But even God cannot interfere with the laws of nature every time some disaster is about to occur. And the all-loving God surely wept with Jill even as he welcomed her daughter into heaven.

In your prayer, reflect on what Jesus told his listeners:

"Are not two sparrows sold for a penny? Yet not one of them will fall to the ground unperceived by your Father. And even the hairs of your head are all counted. So do not be afraid; you are of more value than many sparrows." (Matthew 10:29–31)

Relax in the hand of the God who watches over the tiniest birds. Ask that God to help you believe that divine care still envelops the person you loved and lost far better than you ever could.

Pray for the wisdom to accept that you did the best you could with what you knew, and ask the God of Peace to give comfort to your heart.

. . . . .

When "If Only" Haunts You

My friend Alice was happily married and the mother of two small boys when Tim died suddenly. "We both were so young," she told me. "Of course we thought we had years and years ahead of us. What I have instead is a lot of regrets. If only we had taken that vacation he dreamed of instead of waiting until the boys were older. If only I had spent more time just sitting with him instead of keeping so busy with less important things. If only I had been with him in the emergency room so I could at least have said good-bye. On and on my list goes...."

Most of us have excellent 20/20 hindsight. Had we but known then what we know now, we'd have done many things differently. Death's interruption of a relationship can leave a lot of words unspoken and just as many good intentions unfulfilled. And that's not true only when death is sudden. Even when it has long been expected, it sneaks up on us at the last minute.

And unlike some children's games, life doesn't offer a chance to do it over. Like Alice, you may be haunted by a long list of regrets beginning with "if only."

Someone once quipped that time keeps the world tidy because it keeps everything from happening at once. Maybe that's true, but the downside is that you cannot turn back the clock and make something you missed out on happen again. Instead of going over the what-ifs, try focusing on the fact the beloved person you have buried has escaped the limits of time entirely.

Begin your prayer by reflecting on this promise:

Death will be no more;
mourning and crying and pain will be no more,
for the first things have passed away.
...
"See, I am making all things new." (Revelation 21:4, 5)

This passage describes the world's rebirth at the end of time. Your loved one has already passed beyond time into that realm where God dries every tear and "what if" no longer exists. Simply speak your love. Say all the things you wish you had said when he or she was still in this world with you. And ask for the ability to trust that God even now holds you both together in divine love and in the love you have shared.

· · · · ·

When You Remember Your Failures

Spring break came two months after Susan's mom died. When Susan came home, she was amazed at how empty the house seemed. She said to her dad, "I never realized what a presence Mom was here. I used to complain that she never had an unspoken thought, but now the quiet is deafening!"

Hank nodded in agreement. "We always joked that she did all the talking for both of us," he replied. "And she said that I did all the listening."

"You sure did!" Susan exclaimed. "I could always talk to you and know you'd listen to anything I had to say. Mom used to cut me off at the pass and run her own mouth. Somehow I could never get in sync with her, and I feel really bad about that now that she's dead. I know she loved me, but she always seemed to want something from me that I just couldn't give. I'm such a failure as a daughter!"

Hank put his arms around Susan and held her tight. "I haven't found that to be true," he murmured to her. "And your mom was so proud of you!"

We all fail the people we love at least occasionally. That's what happens when neither partner in a relationship is perfect —and perfection is not exactly a common trait in human beings.

If your failures haunt you, make a conscious effort to turn your mind to the better memories, for a few golden moments creep into even the most strained relationships. Mine other people's memories, for their perception may be as different from yours as Hank's was from Susan's. And the real truth is that we are sometimes clumsy or insensitive.

Find comfort in this admission Saint Paul made about his own inner conflict: "I do not understand my own actions. For I do not do what I want, but I do the very thing I hate.... I can will what is right, but I cannot do it. For I do not do the good I want, but the evil I do not want is what I do" (Romans 7:15, 18–19).

Remembering that this great apostle to the Gentiles ranks high among the saints, turn to him in your prayer. Tell him about the failures that torture you. Ask him to strengthen your belief in the power of God's grace, the belief he clung to with all his might. Feel that grace flooding your whole being. And know that the person you loved so however imperfectly looks on you with the same graciousness.

·　·　·　·　·

When You Think You're Being Punished

Greg and Margie had seven children; now they have four. The first died in his late teens after a long struggle with leukemia. The second succumbed to breast cancer when her first baby was only six months old. The third, a young man just a year out of college, died in an auto accident.

Needless to say, many friends and neighbors gathered for each of the funerals and kept in close touch with the couple as they grieved. But the third death was a bit too much for Margie; she sank into depression for many months.

"What terrible thing have I done that God should punish me so harshly?" she kept asking. The people who knew her well insisted that she had done nothing to deserve such loss, but their words failed to help. Finally one day, a friend answered her question with another: "God who?"

That answer caught Margie completely off guard. All she could say was, "*Huh?*"

"I'm serious," her friend insisted. "What kind of God do you think we're dealing with here? The God I know doesn't punish people without reason. Go back and read your Bible until you can believe what it says a thousand times: that God is kind and merciful and loving!"

Well, maybe not quite a thousand times, but Scripture does repeat the theme of God's love and mercy many, many times. Think back on the readings you have heard in church. What picture of God have they consistently presented? A harsh disciplinarian who beats a child for the slightest offense? Or a tender and loving parent who holds a weeping youngster until the child feels better?

If you feel that your loss is somehow God's punishment, focus on that friend's question, "God who?"

Begin and end your every prayer with the lovely words of the ancient psalmist until you recover your faith in the God described there:

The LORD is gracious and merciful,
   slow to anger and abounding in steadfast love.
The LORD is good to all,
   and his compassion is over all that he has made. (Psalm 145:8–9)

When You Want to Apologize to the Dead

Zach was almost seventeen and his relationship with his dad, Jeff, was typically stormy. One Friday evening he was about to go out to a movie when Jeff made a critical remark about what his son was wearing. A few minutes later they were exchanging verbal blows when Zach stormed out the door.

Later that evening came the knock on the door every parent dreads. Zach had died instantly when a drunk driver struck his car head-on.

His parents made it through the funeral and seemed to be doing as well as could be expected through the next month or two. When the trial date for the driver of the other car came up, Zach's mom, Kerry, wanted to attend, but her husband was dead set against going to the courthouse.

"I just want to hear that man say he's sorry for taking Zach from us," Kerry insisted. "Surely he owes us that much."

"And what do I owe?" Jeff countered. "I was yelling at him about those ratty jeans when he left. I'd give anything to tell him how sorry I am that the last words he heard from me were angry ones."

It really hurts when you want to say you're sorry and the person to whom you want to apologize isn't there to hear you. How can you get rid of the guilt when there is no way left to atone for your mistakes?

Obviously, you can't expect a forgiving hug in this world. But however vast the gulf that separates you from the one to whom you want to apologize, there is one place where you still meet constantly: in the hands of God.

Before you begin your prayer, reflect for a while on these words from Scripture:

But the souls of the righteous are in the hand of God,
and no torment will ever touch them.

In the eyes of the foolish they seemed to have died,
and their departure was thought to be a disaster,
and their going from us to be their destruction;
but they are at peace. (Wisdom of Solomon 3:1–3)

Hold fast to the thought that your loved one is at peace, untroubled by your unresolved quarrel. Write a letter to that person, expressing your painful lack of peace. Tell her or him how very sorry you are, what you would like to be able to do to heal the breach if that were possible.

Give your letter to the person who is in God's hand. In some safe place (outside, perhaps, or over the kitchen sink), light it with a match and watch the smoke from your burnt offering rise toward heaven. Ask God for the grace to believe that your beloved dead has received your apology and is now smiling down at you.

. . . . .

When You Weren't There

Marcella died slowly and painfully of breast cancer. Her husband Bernie suffered every bit as much as she did. He found it excruciating to see her in pain and to watch her slowly decline. After spending nearly half a century with her, he simply could not imagine a life without her.

There were practical reasons for his distress as well. Theirs was a marriage that was more common in previous generations. He provided for all their material needs, working long and hard hours. She in turn took care of him just as thoroughly as his mother had many years earlier. She cooked his meals, washed his laundry and every evening laid out the clothes he would wear to work the next day. Each of them was completely dependent on the other.

Finally she went into hospice care. As the inevitability of her imminent death became too obvious for either of them to ignore, he began to plead with her not to leave him. He kept asking how she thought he was going to manage without her—over and over again. One evening Marcella told him to go home and get some rest. "I'm tired too," she said. "I'll be asleep before you get to the elevator."

A bit reluctantly, Bernie left. And Marcella did go to sleep—a sleep from which she never awoke.

Weeks after the funeral, Bernie was still berating himself for having left. "I should have been with her!" he sobbed. "I never should have left her to die without my hand to hold." Finally his son spoke up. "Dad," he said, "didn't she tell you to go home?"

"Yes, but—," Bernie's sentence was interrupted by his son.

"Dad, maybe she found it as hard to leave you as you found it to let her go. I think maybe she just wanted to slip away quietly to spare you."

There is no easy way to say good-bye to someone you love. Whether death arrives without warning or after a long and difficult struggle, this parting is wholly unlike the other separations you have known. The tenderest words of farewell cannot lessen the pain either for the living who must stay behind or for the dying who must leave. Yet there is no way to avoid it. The moment will inevitably come for each of us. Even God's own Son could not escape death when he became human. And the friends who watched him die had no opportunity to say good-bye. Perhaps the person who felt the pain of the moment most keenly was the person who gave birth to him: Mary.

Recall the scene depicted in this brief Scripture passage: "Meanwhile, standing near the cross of Jesus were his mother, and his mother's sister, Mary the wife of Clopas, and Mary Magdalene" (John 19:25).

Imagine how Mary must have felt watching her son suffer and die. Turn to that grieving mother in your prayer. Recall to mind the poignant sculpture the great Michelangelo carved five centuries ago, the Pietà. (Maybe there is a reproduction of it in your own church. You can surely find a picture of it in any encyclopedia or perhaps even in your dictionary.) See the sorrow in the woman's face as she gazes at the lifeless Son lying across her lap.

Remember that Mary's Son rose from the dead in just three days, but she did not realize that was about to happen as she held his body. You know you and your loved one will meet again because Jesus has promised it. Ask Mary to strengthen you in that belief. Recall that her dying Son bequeathed his mother to his followers from the cross. Ask Mary to weep with you and for you as you struggle with your loss.

. . . . .

When You Wish You'd Been More Loving

I first met Jim when I took Communion to him and his wife, Ann. It was Ann who couldn't get to church. Once she died, Jim began to show up regularly, settling himself into the pew beside me.

It had been a while since I talked to Jim, and I was beginning to worry about him. So I called him. I was right to worry about not seeing him for awhile; he had been ill.

Our conversation settled, as always, on his love for Ann, his wife of well over half a century. She had been a beauty, a model, in fact.

During our conversation, Jim was being a little hard on himself. He kept going back to the times he had let Ann down (or so he thought), those moments when he had not been as loving as perhaps he could have been.

"You had fifty-seven years together, right?" I asked him. He verified the number, and I asked another question: "And in all that time you weren't perfect every minute?"

"Of course not," he granted. "But now I wish I had been."

"Ann was a wonderful person," I said truthfully. "But was she perfect?"

"Not quite," Jim admitted.

The only one who manages to be perfectly loving every minute of every day is God. The rest of us muddle through as well as our flawed humanity allows. But sometimes our failures cause us deep regret—especially when someone we have dearly loved is beyond our reach. What we then tend to forget is that the loved one wasn't perfect, either. Yet that person managed to overlook our failures, just as we paid only a little attention to his or hers.

Reflect on this Scripture passage: "Beloved, we are God's children now; what we will be has not yet been revealed. What we do know is this: when he is revealed, we will be like him, for we will see him as he is" (1 John 3:2-3).

The late Franciscan Father Leonard Foley once wrote that heaven is a place where we will all be able to love perfectly. And that is what this passage promises, for John later insists that God *is* love (see 1 John 4:8). Think of the person you loved so dearly but imperfectly as now capable of loving you as God does: perfectly. And know that none of your failures are held against you by that person. Bask in the warmth of his or her acceptance until you are able to forgive yourself.

part five

PRAYING

YOUR

WAY

THROUGH

DEPRESSION

When People Tell You to Get Over It

Marta has been a widow for many months now, and she is getting mighty tired of hurting. "It's no longer a constant ache that demands all my attention," she says. "Rather, it sneaks up on me. I'm going about doing what I have to do, and suddenly I think of Terry and a wave of sorrow sweeps over me. Worst of all, there's no longer anyone I can talk to about the way I feel. Terry was only forty when a massive coronary took him from me in an instant. The people closest to me are still happily married; there are no other widows in my circle of friends. The same folks who were so wonderfully supportive when Terry died are now telling me that it's time to pull myself together and get on with my life. How I wish I could!"

Deep wounds heal slowly. Few of us would argue about that when the wound is physical. But people who are wounded emotionally often find themselves surrounded by people who want to see them heal more quickly—and are themselves impatient with how long it takes. Grieving normally lasts a least a year, and often longer. There's a good reason for that: Every turn of a calendar page brings a new date whose significance tears at your heart. And, since you were probably pretty numb at the outset of your grief, you may not yet have worked through a lot of important dates.

Remind the people who are telling you to "get over it" that they would not rush you through, for example, the loss of a leg. They would patiently allow you time for the wound to heal and for an artificial limb to be fitted, plus the lengthy time in therapy you would need to learn how to walk on a foot that cannot feel the ground. Point out that you have indeed lost a part of yourself—and please pass the tissues!

In your prayer, ask for the grace to be patient with yourself, just as God has ever and always been patient with you. Reflect on these ancient words from Scripture: "Thus says the LORD, the God of your ancestor David: I have heard your prayer, I have seen your tears; indeed, I will heal you" (2 Kings 20:5).

. . . . .

When You Always Feel Tired

"When I get up in the morning, I am already tired," Carl complains. "I drag myself off to work and struggle to make it through the day. I get home and I'm too tired to think about a decent meal, so I grab a handful of nuts and collapse in front of the TV until it gets to be a reasonable time for bed. I am *so* tired of being tired!"

Grieving can be like carrying a heavy boulder around all day long. The weight of it is a constant demand on your energy and your strength. The weariness you feel is a classic symptom of depression. Had it come upon you suddenly and without reason, you'd head straight for your doctor. But your loss is a wound that medical science cannot cure.

It will heal, in spite of the fact that the pain seems to go on forever. In the meantime, be gentle with yourself. Keep your expectations low; this is no time to tackle something as difficult as, say, a move. You can't run away from mourning; trying only adds more stress to your life.

Take your weariness to Jesus in your prayer. Reflect on his invitation: "Come to me, all you that are weary and are carrying heavy burdens, and I will give you rest. Take my yoke upon you, and learn from me; for I am gentle and humble in heart, and you will find rest for your souls" (Matthew 11:28–29).

Most of us who live in a mechanized world have never seen a yoke. In the Israel of Jesus' time, it was a familiar sight, for it is a bar that lies across the shoulders of two side-by-side draft animals, teaming their strength against the drag of a heavy load.

By inviting us to put his yoke on our shoulders, Jesus is *not* imposing another burden on us. Rather, he is offering to help us carry the load that is weighing us down. And he has already made good on that promise, for the Son of God took on human flesh and shared our pain and sorrow. He wept at the death of his friend Lazarus; he stretched out his arms and died on the cross, abandoned by most of his friends.

Lay your weary head on his shoulder and accept his offer to help you carry your load of grief—not just once, but over and over again whenever your strength fails.

. . . . .

When You Can't Accomplish Anything

"At the end of every day, my list of things I meant to do was just as long as it was when I got up in the morning. My inability to get anything done just depressed me more. In desperation I decided to make a list of the things I did manage to do each day. Sometimes there was nothing on it but 'got out of bed; ate breakfast.' But focusing on what I had done, no matter how small, was more helpful than beating myself up for what I hadn't accomplished," remarked Jerry.

If you feel overwhelmed by all you have to do, and even more so, by all that you haven't done, start keeping a list like Jerry's. At the end of each day, give thanks to God for giving you the strength to do whatever you have done, no matter how small. To help you remember that God treasures even the smallest act, especially if it costs dearly, reflect on this incident in the life of Jesus:

[Jesus] sat down opposite the treasury, and watched the crowd putting money into the treasury. Many rich people put in large sums. A poor widow came and put in two small copper coins, which are worth a penny. Then he called his disciples and said to them, "Truly I tell you, this poor widow has put in more than all those who are contributing to the treasury. For all of them have contributed out of their abundance; but she out of her poverty has put in everything... she had to live on. (Mark 12:41–44)

Perhaps the one thing you might try to do today is to make some gesture of sympathy and support to another person who is weighed down by sorrow or trouble, however small that gesture may be. You'll be surprised at how much better it makes you feel.

. . . . .

When You Can't Even Pray

When someone is having a really tough time, my friend Theresa always promises to pray for that person. That's usually a welcome offer, for hurting people know they need all the prayers they can get. But Theresa means something more. "I don't mean just that I will pray for you," she explains. "I know how hard it is to pray when everything is going wrong, so I'll pray in your stead. I'll be your designated pray-er."

That's an unusual spin on what it means to pray for someone. But there is biblical precedent for Theresa's offer. When the Hebrews escaped from Egypt, they faced many difficulties in their long journey across the desert. Just before they reached Mt. Sinai, where Moses would receive the commandments from God, at one time they came under attack by a fierce tribe called the Amalekites. Here's how the book of Exodus tells the story:

Moses said to Joshua, "Choose some men for us and go out; fight with Amalek. Tomorrow I will stand on top of the hill with the staff of God in my hand." So Joshua did as Moses told him, and fought with Amalek, while Moses, Aaron, and Hur went up to the top of the hill. Whenever Moses held up his hand, Israel prevailed; and whenever he lowered his hand, Amalek prevailed. But Moses' hands grew weary; so they took a stone and put it under him, and he sat on it. Aaron and Hur held up his hands, one on one side, and the other on the other side; so his hands were steady until the sun set. And Joshua defeated Amalek... (Exodus 17:9–13)

Explain to the friends who offer their prayers for you how much difficulty you are having in praying. Tell them what Theresa says to her friends and about what Moses' friends did for him. Ask them to support the arms you have such difficulty raising in prayer.

. . . . .

When You Can't Stop Crying

"The numbness I felt for the first few weeks after Joe died didn't *wear* off," Judy says. "It was *washed* out by a flood of tears. Anything could set me off. I'd wake up in the morning and remember he was dead, and the tears would start. I'd run across a note he had written to himself and the sight of his handwriting made me cry. Getting caught in a traffic jam, having trouble opening a jar, a broken fingernail—the slightest frustration was enough to open the floodgates. I constantly made other people uncomfortable and embarrassed myself, but I just couldn't stop crying."

Tears are a normal response to great sorrow. According to a story in Jewish folklore, God felt a twinge of pity as Adam and Eve trudged sadly out of the garden. The creator stopped them and pressed into their hands a pearl out of the heavenly treasury. "This is a tear," God explained. "When sorrow and pain overwhelm you, it will fall from your eyes. Your burden will then be lighter."

Tears are indeed a gift from God. According to medical science, they contain a chemical that is a natural pain reliever. You may protest that crying doesn't make you feel better at all. It just makes your eyes puffy and your nose stuffy.

To make matters worse, you know that your tears upset the people who care about you. But don't let them tell you to stop because unshed tears are much harder on you. They eat away at your stomach and stress your entire body. So go ahead and give yourself permission to cry, even if no one else will.

Begin your prayer with the psalmist's complaint:

I am weary with my moaning;
   every night I flood my bed with tears;
   I drench my couch with my weeping.
My eyes waste away because of grief.... (Psalm 6:6–7)

Give thanks to God for the compassionate gift of tears. And trust that the heart of the loving God who throughout history has taken pity on sorrowing people aches with you and for you.

. . . . .

When You Feel Helpless

My father-in-law had never even fixed his own breakfast before his wife became seriously ill. But after she died, he was determined to conquer the kitchen. Picture Don Quixote charging those windmills! I regularly got what we soon termed "Dial-a-Cook" calls: "How do you mince an onion? This recipe calls for oil; what kind does it mean? How do you bake a potato?"

It's not easy to learn the skills someone else put at your service for half a century. Dad never did manage to get a whole meal together at the same time. Until he moved into a retirement home, he'd fix one food at a time: first his meat, then his potato.... But there was at last a family Thanksgiving gathering for which he made the pumpkin pies—and no prouder a chef ever ruled in a four-star restaurant!

Some couples start out with a clear plan for dividing responsibilities; others simply fall into the habit. But the death of one is sure to leave the other floundering with some unfamiliar task. An old dog can indeed learn new tricks, but there's nothing easy about it. It is no fun to feel helpless and inept, even when the struggle finally yields to competence.

If you are struggling with such learning, be as patient with yourself as you would with a child trying to master a new skill. All of us were born helpless—and we often screamed with rage at our situation when we were tiny.

Trust yourself to the most loving parent of all, the God who formed you. Reflect on the words an ancient prophet spoke for Israel's God:

When Israel was a child, I loved him,
    and out of Egypt I called my son.
. . .
Yet it was I who taught Ephraim to walk,
    I took them up in my arms;
. . .
I was to them like those
    who lift infants to their cheeks.
    I bent down to them and fed them. (Hosea 11:1, 3, 4)

. . . . .

When You Feel Overwhelmed

Everything was going well for Ben and Helen. Their small business was getting off to a good start; they had two bright and healthy children and a loving marriage. Then one sunny Sunday afternoon, Ben and a friend were enjoying a game of tennis when a sudden heart attack left Ben lying dead on the court. "I wasn't sure I could make it through the funeral," Helen says. "But that was the easiest part. Then I suddenly found myself bearing all the responsibility for the kids by myself and trying to keep the business running at the same time. I thought I'd lose my mind.

"Dinnertime was the absolute bottom of the day. I'd come home from work too tired to cook, and the kids were at that picky stage where all they wanted to eat was a burger and fries. I never wanted to see another hamburger as long as I lived!

"One day I said as much to a neighbor who asked how I was doing. The next day she showed up with a kid-friendly casserole. The day after that another neighbor invited us to join them for dinner. The meals and invitations kept on coming at least three or four times every week after that. I still miss Ben enormously, but I am wrapped in so much care that I'm beginning to feel almost on top of things again."

Losing someone upon whom you always relied for help and support is bound to leave you feeling overwhelmed by the responsibilities you now bear alone. When your loss was raw and new, many people told you to let them know if there was anything they could do. Maybe you could suggest something. More likely, you just realized that they couldn't do the one thing you wanted the most: restore your loved one to you.

As time goes by, you hear that question less, but friends and neighbors are still more than willing to lend a hand if you need one. Helen discovered that purely by accident when she expressed her frustration to a neighbor who quickly picked up on her need. But you can still ask for help. Before you dismiss that suggestion out of hand, ask how you would respond to such a request from someone in your situation. As generously as you could, right?

In your prayer, borrow the words of the psalmist:

Save me, O God,
for the waters have come up to my neck.
I sink in deep mire,
where there is no foothold;
I have come into deep waters,
and the flood sweeps over me. (Psalm 69:1–2)

Ask God to guide you to someone who can lend a hand and lighten your burdens. Don't expect to hear the divine voice thundering from a cloud; just look around you. Call to mind the people who supported you when your loss was fresh. Hear again the voices who told you to let them know if there was anything they could do.

Take the offers seriously, no matter how much time has passed. Remind them of their generous words, and admit that you didn't know then how anything could help in the face of your loss. Admit what you are now having difficulty coping with, and see if they can give you a hand.

And, of course, remember to thank God for sending generous hearts your way.

. . . . .

When You Feel Alone

Many churches, my own among them, offer a special service not long before Christmas, a prayer experience for people who find the holidays especially difficult because of some great sorrow in their lives. This year, far too many people I know attended—the same folks whose loved one's funerals I had attended in the months before.

"It was good to be there," one of them told me. "For the first time in months I didn't feel so alone. I still miss my husband, of course, but at least I realize that I'm not the only person who is mourning instead of rejoicing this holiday season. It was such a comfort to pray with people who are no more in a 'ho-ho-ho' mood than I am."

Grief can be isolating, especially when you are surrounded by people who have something to be excited and happy about. However sympathetic they may be, they can't imagine the raw hurt you feel unless they have been through a significant loss themselves. (How well did you understand before your own loss?)

Some people find a support group of some sort a lifeline as they work through their grief. Others prefer not to listen to other people's sad stories. But praying with someone whose prayer rises from the same needs and feelings as yours is a good way to ease your loneliness.

Consider reaching out to someone else who is recently bereaved with a pact to pray with and for one another. Or, since prayer is not bound by normal human limitations, turn to someone who is too far away to meet with. Enlist the support of someone who lives miles away or even someone who is no longer living at all. My grandmother, for instance, lost her first-born daughter at the age of six weeks. When I gave birth to a very premature baby whose life hung delicately in the balance, guess to whom I turned? Nobody could understand better than my grandmother why I wanted to get to know this baby and watch her grow up.

Let Jesus' own promise spur your intention. Recall what he said about supporting one another in prayer: "Again, truly I tell you, if two of you agree on earth about anything you ask, it will be done for you by my Father in heaven. For where two or three are gathered in my name, I am there among them" (Matthew 18:19–20).

When You Just Want to Be Alone

"I'm just not good company these days," Dick admits. "I have no patience with small talk. I've forgotten what it feels like to care about who won the big game or even the local election. My friends keep inviting me to go out with them or to come over for a meal. They know I am hurting, and I really appreciate their concern. But I find it very hard to be with them. Katie and I had so many good times with these folks, and being with them just makes her absence throb more painfully.

"I know they don't understand why I'd rather stay home alone. I'm probably hurting their feelings, but I can't help it. I just can't hack their company right now."

The death of someone with whom you have shared a life upsets the balance of many relationships. Like Dick, you may find yourself uncomfortable in the old circles of friends and relatives. Those once-familiar havens become painful reminders of your loss, and you want to avoid them.

It's perfectly OK to seek a bit of solitude. Extroverts will never understand this, but introverts like me cherish alone time! Even if you have always been happier in the company of others, your grief, like Dick's, may make you want to get away even from people whose company you have long enjoyed. Give yourself permission to say no to company.

And in your prayer, remember that Jesus, that lover of company, sought solitude when he was facing the ordeal of Good Friday. (For that matter, he often went off to pray in a lonely place, according to the Gospels.) Reflect on these words that describe one of the most difficult moments of his life:

[Jesus] came out and went, as was his custom, to the Mount of Olives; and the disciples followed him. When he reached the place, he said to them, "Pray that you may not come into the time of trial." Then he withdrew from them about a stone's throw, knelt down, and prayed.... In his anguish he prayed more earnestly, and his sweat became like great drops of blood falling down on the ground. (Luke 22:39–41, 44)

Following your Lord's example, give yourself permission to avoid company when their companionship only increases the pain of your loss. Remember that when Jesus went off to be alone, it was to pray. In your solitude, turn to the Lord who also sometimes sought to avoid company. Ask him to help you find the comfort you so desperately seek.

. . . . .

When You Just Want to Stay in Bed
One bright, sunny afternoon Jo's eleven-year-old son set out on his bike and headed for a friend's house. He never got there. A car swerved when another driver made an abrupt lane change and struck Zach's rear wheel. The boy was thrown to the pavement and died instantly.

"The whole world just turned black in an instant," Jo says. "I could hardly put one foot in front of the other. The hardest part of all was getting out of bed in the morning. To get to the kitchen I had to walk past Zach's bedroom. Even though I kept the door closed, I could still see his empty bed. I just wanted to pull the covers over my head and never get up again."

If you have the same longing to avoid facing the new day, indulge yourself. Hit the snooze alarm and pull the covers over your head. Curl up and imagine yourself back in your mother's womb. It is dark, but it is not quiet. You can hear a beating heart, rhythmic and soothing. Soon enough you will have to leave this space and make the terrifying journey through the birth canal. You will emerge gasping; you will expel the strange air from your lungs with a cry and close your eyes against the bright light. But soon you will be in your mother's arms, listening again to the familiar sound of her beating heart.

When the alarm sounds again, ease yourself out from under the covers. And carry with you into the day the words of the prophet:

> Can a woman forget her nursing-child,
>> or show no compassion for the child of her womb?
> Even these may forget,
>> yet I will not forget you. (Isaiah 49:15)

. . . . .

When You Wish You Had Died Instead

One rainy evening, Julie was driving her oldest child, fourteen-year-old Tim, to basketball practice. As she went through an intersection, another vehicle zoomed through the stop sign and crashed into the side of her car. Neither Julie nor the other driver was seriously injured, thanks to front air bags. But Tim was dead when the police arrived.

Needless to say, Julie was devastated. And her pain only increased in the months following the boy's death. "Why wasn't I killed instead of Tim?" she kept asking. "He had his whole life before him."

One day her husband couldn't take it anymore. "What are you saying?" Bill asked. "My heart is broken, too. But we have three other children. What would they do without you? What would I do without you? Can you really think any of us—Tim included—would be better off if you were dead?"

Ask yourself the same question: Would the person you loved so dearly be better off without you? Would you want that person to feel the pain that is now tearing at your heart? Chances are that your love for the other would make you want to protect her or him from the heartache of loss no less than you wish you could have prevented the death that claimed your loved one.

In your prayer, reflect on the story of Israel's great King David, from whom Jesus traced his human descent. David's family was a troubled one, to say the least. Not long after David became king, a bitter quarrel between two of his sons, Amnon and Absalom, led the latter to arrange the other's murder. David, who loved both his sons, could not completely reconcile with Absalom, and the young man plotted to seize his father's throne. David sent his men to quell the rebellion but cautioned them not to harm Absalom. The unfortunate young man got himself tangled in the branch of a tree and accidentally strangled.

When he heard the news, David wept inconsolably: "O my son Absalom, my son, my son Absalom! Would I had died instead of you, O Absalom, my son, my son!" (2 Samuel 18:33).

Picture the one you loved grieving for you, echoing David's cry just as you have done. Try to feel grateful that it is only happening in your imagination. Ask God to help you bear your loss; thank God, if you can, for the pain your loved one has been spared.

And now my soul is poured out within me;
    days of affliction have taken hold of me.
The night racks my bones,
    and the pain that gnaws me takes no rest. (Job 30:16–17)

part six

PRAYING

YOUR

WAY

TO

ACCEPTANCE

Can I Accept God's Will?

My friend Jackie is God's staunch defender. I first saw her in that role many decades ago when we served together on our parish bereavement committee. We were sitting with a family, helping them to plan a funeral liturgy for a teenager who had died suddenly and tragically. One family member was insisting over and over again that they all had to find a way to accept God's will. Finally Jackie looked her straight in the eye and said, "How come we only talk about God's will when terrible things happen?"

Ain't it the truth! Did you ever enjoy one of life's small pleasures—watch a breathtaking sunset or lick an ice cream cone, say—and think of God's will? I'd be willing to bet that phrase didn't come to mind at moments of great joy, either, even though you may have breathed a prayer of thanksgiving.

Let's face facts: God is not a micromanager. If the world were under constant divine control, it would surely be a different place. Nations would live together in peace; no child would ever go to bed hungry, because those who have much would share generously with the folks who have nothing. Things such as these are clearly in harmony with God's will! Ponder these words:

> ...God did not make death,
> and he does not delight in the death of the living.
> For he created all things so that they might exist;
> the generative forces of the world are wholesome,
> and there is no destructive poison in them,
> and the dominion of Hades is not on earth. (Wisdom of Solomon 1:13–14)

See how long a list you can make of the things, both large and small, that have brought you joy. Spend a little time each day thanking God for them until you begin to believe that to shower us with blessings is truly God's will.

. . . . .

Can I Accept the Unacceptable?

My parish asked me to visit a young couple with a seriously ill four-year-old. "Seriously ill" was a gross understatement. Julie had Tay-Sachs disease, a fatal genetic illness that slowly destroys the brain because the lack of some crucial enzyme allows fatty tissue to build up in it. These babies develop normally at first, then start losing ground. By the time I met her she was blind and deaf, partially paralyzed and on a feeding tube because she could no longer swallow. She was also beautiful with thick blond curls and long black lashes around her incredibly blue eyes. She broke *my* heart; you can imagine how she shredded her mom's and dad's.

"How can you live with this?" I asked.

"We have no choice," they replied. "We love her and we will take the best possible care of her as long as she lives."

What those parents suffered was surely unacceptable, yet they had no choice but to accept it. Neither do you have a choice. All any of us has is the certainty that the God whom Jesus called Father shares our pain just as any loving parent does.

Recall how Jesus urged his listeners to trust this God as completely as their children trust them: "Is there anyone among you who, if your child asks for bread, will give a stone? Or if the child asks for a fish, will give a snake?" (Matthew 7:9–10).

Half a century ago the great Protestant theologian Reinhold Niebuhr penned a prayer that has become famous because of its adoption by Alcoholics Anonymous and its spin-off groups. Make the Serenity Prayer your own and repeat it often:

O God,
give me serenity to accept what cannot be changed,
courage to change what should be changed,
and the wisdom to know the difference.

. . . . .

Is There Light at the End of This Tunnel?

My friend Amy lost her five-year-old son many years ago. Now she speaks of the grief she suffered as a long dark tunnel. "For months on end the whole world was all pitch-black," she tells me. "I don't think I ever laughed—and if I did, I felt guilty. How could I think of enjoying myself when my little Timmy was dead? We had laid him deep in the earth where the sun never reached. What made it even worse was that Timmy was afraid of the dark. If he woke during the night, he'd cry until we came and held him. Suddenly I was the one who would wake up in the night and begin to cry.

"When Christmas was getting near that first year after Timmy died, I wasn't sure how I was going to get through it. I started to go to daily Mass in the hope that that would help. The morning of Christmas Eve, the Gospel was about the prophecy Zechariah spoke after he chose a name for his son, John the Baptist. It was a beautiful promise that light would break through the darkness.

"It was a lifeline. I reread it every day for months."

Grief can certainly be as long and dark as an Arctic winter. Like Amy, perhaps you find yourself always feeling lost in the darkness. In your imagination, place yourself in the far northern region of our planet. Imagine living through long months when the sun never comes up at all. Let yourself feel how dark and cold it is.

Then remember that spring does come even to that bleak landscape. Watch the sun finally rise above the horizon—at first for a few minutes, and then a little longer every day until at last it is daylight all around the clock. Read and reflect on the prophecy Zechariah spoke:

> By the tender mercy of our God,
>> the dawn from on high will break upon us,
> to give light to those who sit in darkness and in the shadow of death,
>> to guide our feet into the way of peace. (Luke 1:78–79)

Remember that God keeps promises. In your prayer, speak about how wearying the darkness is, of how you long for the bright light of the sun.

. . . . .

Will I Dare to Love Again?

After living on his own for sometime after my mother-in-law died, my father-in-law moved into a retirement home. He often went to church via the home's bus. One Sunday Dad was unable to get off the bus. The driver took one look at him and called an ambulance. At the age of eighty-five, Dad had emergency triple bypass surgery.

His recovery was long and hard, but he finally returned to the retirement home. When he boarded the bus for church the following Sunday, a woman he knew invited him to sit beside her. Helen had been widowed for many years, and one of the things they had in common was that they had both been married on the same day more than half a century before.

A few months later Dad broke the news to his kids: He and Helen were getting married. "I was afraid everyone would think we're crazy for getting married at our age," he told me. "Dad," I answered, "it's a little crazy at any age."

Surprisingly, that couple had six years together, then died within half an hour of each other. I think one of them must have said, "Come on, honey, it's time to go."

If you have just buried a spouse, I know you're in no mood to think about marrying again—nor am I urging you to. But the simple fact is that having loved and lost anyone dear plants a seed of fear in our hearts. We hesitate to invest so much of ourselves in another person ever again.

But the truth is that we don't "find" love; love finds us. For love's other name is God, and God seeks us out relentlessly. Reflect on this scriptural passage:

> Beloved, let us love one another, because love is from God; everyone who loves is born of God and knows God. Whoever does not love does not know God, for God is love…. Beloved, since God has loved us so much, we also ought to love one another. No one has ever seen God; if we love one another, God lives in us, and his love is perfected in us….
>
> God is love, and those who abide in love abide in God, and God abides in them." (1 John 4:7–8, 11–12, 16)

Call into your prayer—into God's presence with you—the people you have loved most deeply and by whom you have been most dearly loved. Include the one for whom you are mourning, of course. Give thanks for them. And ask yourself how they have shaped you, how they have shaped your image of God.

. . . . .

Will I Ever Learn to Live Without My Loved One?

My grandmother had a great devotion to Saint Anthony of Padua. She kept that patron saint of lost things busy trying to locate whatever anyone mislaid. But she didn't stop there. She could express anything as something she wanted him to find:

a job for someone, a child for an infertile couple. We used to tease her by saying that when she got to heaven, Anthony would name her second in command of the lost and found department.

My dad contracted a terminal illness some years after Gram died. On the Sunday morning of his death, my mother, my sister and I found our way to church. Needless to say, all three of us were wiping tears from our eyes all through the Mass. As we got up to leave at the end of the service, a woman behind us leaned forward and said, "I don't know what is wrong, but I have been praying for you. Here, take these; they may help." She pressed a couple of leaflets into Mother's hand. They were prayers to Saint Anthony! None of us had any doubt who had "found" them for us.

I still ask Gram to find things for me—and she's good. Finding the item that was right there just a minute ago or locating a convenient parking place are no challenge at all for her. She can handle things that are harder to find as well: the hearing aid dropped while weeding a flower bed, a way to stretch the budget just a little farther, the ability to maintain hope in a difficult situation or calm in a crisis.

Who is your favorite saint? Chances are you will name one of the greats, for they are the most familiar to us. But one of the requirements for canonization is *heroic* sanctity. Heaven is crowded mostly with ordinary folks like you and me, people who spent their lives offering small gestures of love—as Gram did for me. These are the folks we honor on the Feast of All Saints, and they are no less devoted to interceding for us than the famous folks.

Reflect on the words of Jesus: "Come, you that are blessed by my Father, inherit the kingdom prepared for you from the foundation of the world; for I was hungry and you gave me food, I was thirsty and you gave me something to drink..." (Matthew 25:34–35).

Recall the uncanonized folks who have blessed your life with love and healing and forgiveness. Thank God for bringing these saints your way. And pray a litany that includes not only the heroes and heroines of our faith, but also those who simply blessed your life. Be sure to include the one for whom you mourn, for that person undoubtedly still cares about your needs and watches over you.

.   .   .   .   .

Will I Ever Understand What God Wants of Me?

My Aunt Honora was fairy godmother to three generations of nieces and nephews, all of whom loved her dearly. So, when she was hospitalized after a heart attack, my sister flew across the country to be with her. I made the same trip when she went home. While I was there, she took a sudden turn for the worse and died. I knew she had long ago made funeral arrangements, so I called the funeral home. They told me to bring her social security card when I came to finalize the funeral plans.

Back at her apartment, I went looking for it. I found it easily enough in her wallet, but I found something else, too: a photo of a young Honora with a young man in uniform. I was completely baffled. You see, she had never married—had never, to my knowledge, even had a serious interest in anyone.

As I phoned the news of her death to the rest of the family, her younger sister, my Aunt Louise, told me the story only she had ever known. She had introduced Nonie (as we knew her) to a young marine, and they fell in love. But World War II broke out, and Nonie's marine went to the Far East, where he died in a Japanese prison camp.

The truth is that we never really get over a loss. We *accept* it, but that doesn't mean we like it. It only means that we realize we cannot change what has happened. The wound heals. Although we still bear the scar, we begin to build a new life without someone important. And that life can be surprisingly rich.

That was certainly true of Nonie. She never forgot her loss, and kept that photo in her wallet until she was ninety. For many decades she lavished the love she would have given her marine and any children they might have had on three generations of nieces and nephews. And we were certainly much the richer for it! She did exactly what God wants each of us to do: Love generously.

Remember that the Risen Christ is always depicted with scarred hands. Put yourself in the Upper Room with the disciples and hear Jesus invite you as he invited Thomas to see the wounds in his palms. Listen to him explain that the marks he still bears testify to his love for you.

Remember what he told his friends at the Last Supper: "I give you a new commandment, that you love one another. Just as I have loved you, you also should love one another. By this everyone will know that you are my disciples, if you have love for one another" (John 13:34–35).

Ask the scarred Lord to help you lavish the love you had for the person who has died on the living people who still need it.

.   .   .   .   .

Will I Find Happiness Again?

Carolyn looked up from the book she was reading to the little grandson on her lap. "Did you ever notice," she asked her daughter, Jenny, "how all the stories we read to children have a happy ending? Sometimes I think we're not preparing them very well for life. The wolf may eat Grandma; Cinderella's coach might never be anything more than a pumpkin; when Jack chops down the beanstalk, the giant may land on him and crush him."

"Aren't you in a jolly frame of mind!" Jenny remarked. "What brought all that on?"

"Your dad's death, I guess," Carolyn replied. "I just find it very hard to believe in happy endings anymore. I can't imagine that I'll ever be really happy again."

Grief does that to all of us. It lasts such a very long time, and every time we think we're getting over it, we find ourselves right back at square one. It gets very hard to believe that someday we will not only be happy again, we will also consider it a normal state to be in once more.

The *Zohar*, one of the books produced by the Jewish tradition of interpretation known as *kabalah*, says that only someone with a broken heart is a whole person because only such a heart makes room for the presence of God. This tradition rose a thousand years after Jesus' time, yet he said much the same thing in the Sermon on the Mount. He pronounced what we call the Beatitudes, naming as blessed the very folks we think of as unfortunate. "Blessed are those who mourn," he said, "for they will be comforted" (Matthew 5:4).

Some people make a career out of searching for happiness, but that is a vain quest. For it seems to be the nature of happiness to find us, even to catch us off guard. For we are most likely to be happy when we are drawn out of ourselves, when we forget our desire to be happy and turn our attention more to bringing joy to others. In other words, happiness is born of the serenity that comes with acceptance of whatever is.

Reread the Beatitudes (Matthew 5:1–11) as a springboard to prayer. Imagine yourself sitting on that hillside listening to Jesus' voice as he speaks them. See his face turning directly to you as he talks, and ask him to help you grasp fully the meaning of his words.

. . . . .

Will I Find a Happy Ending?

My grandmother's first child died at the age of six weeks. Although she and her husband Tom had three more children, they continued to think of Ruthie as part of their family for the rest of their lives. Not only their other children but also their grandchildren (including me) had heard about this beautiful infant as long as they could remember.

Grace outlived Tom by many years. In her old age she developed dementia. My children remember her as the funny old lady who babbled like a toddler just learning to talk. Only two times in the last five years of her life did she say anything rational.

The first time was when she was hospitalized for some ailment. One day a nurse complimented her on how pretty she looked. "Your boyfriend must be coming today," the woman teased. Gram stiffened and retorted, "My boyfriend has been dead for ten years!" (She may have missed by a year or so.)

The other occasion was when she drawing close to death. Suddenly she looked at the wall and cried out quite clearly: "Look, there's Tom. And he's holding little Ruthie!" And then she went to join them.

The Joyful Mysteries are the events Mary treasured in her heart, just as my grandmother treasured the memories of her husband and their firstborn. Look up the passages underlying those mysteries and notice how many of them have a bittersweet edge. The first, the Annunciation (Luke 1:26–35), presented Mary with a tough problem. How was she going to explain her pregnancy to her family and neighbors, to say

79

nothing of Joseph? The third, the familiar story of Jesus' birth (Luke 2:2–7), includes a long and hard journey for a woman heavy with child and a birth in a rude stable. The fourth, the Presentation in the Temple (Luke 2:22–38), includes a warning that Mary's heart will be pierced. The last, the Finding of Jesus in the Temple (Luke 2:41–50), ends for Joseph and Mary with bewilderment at Jesus' remarks. Only the second mystery, the Visitation (Luke 1:39–56), seems to be purely joyful.

Make your personal list of joyful mysteries, the precious moments you hold in your heart. Recalling them will make your heart ache now, but these are the treasures you will keep. Like Mary, reflect on them in spite of your pain and confusion, and thank God that you have them.

. . . . .

Will I Find Out Who I Am Now?

I claim a sizable group of now middle-aged women as my "other daughters." Some of them even call me "mom." I am Grandma Carol to some children.

The relationships go back many years. The first were neighbors' kids. I taught them to sew, attended their orchestra concerts, celebrated their triumphs and listened to their frustrations with a non-parental ear. Later acquisitions were young women I mentored at work. To them I became the "staff mom." I never questioned why I thought of them as daughters.

When my parish first organized volunteers into service to the needs of our members, I signed up for the bereavement committee. Much of what I have published over the years is directed either to sorrowing people or to the folks who minister to them. I never wondered about that choice of direction either.

And then one day the daughter I had surrendered to adoptive

parents as an infant found me. Once I had dealt with the grief I had never allowed myself to feel, the reason for the choices I made slowly became apparent. The hole giving up that baby had left in my heart had created ample room for other nurturing relationships. The loss I had never mourned had made me more sensitive to the sorrows of others. The best parts of me, I discovered, are formed from my scar tissue.

Spend some time thinking back over the hardships you have known over the years. Ask yourself how they changed you. Did you gain new strengths or acquire greater sensitivities from those experiences?

Ask God to help you trust that the loss you are now mourning will bring the same graced results. And slowly pray the words of the psalmist:

O LORD, you have searched me and known me.
. . .
You hem me in, behind and before,
  and lay your hand upon me.
. . .
For it was you who formed my inward parts;
  you knit me together in my mother's womb.
I praise you, for I am fearfully and wonderfully made.
  Wonderful are your works;
that I know very well. (Psalm 139:1, 5, 13–14)

.   .   .   .   .

Will I Learn to Let Go?

"My mother was a control freak. She didn't like me to make any choice on my own, even when I was an adult with children of my own." Andi shakes her head sadly. "Without a good role model to follow, motherhood was something I groped my way through. Then one day I found a wonderful role model, a woman who wrote an article in which she said that some things can only be held with open hands. She used filling your hands with water as an example. If you close them, of course the water runs right out. But if you keep them gently cupped, you can fill your palms.

"So I tried to apply that with my kids. And I think I did a pretty good job of it. I let them take a lot of risks. I sent them away to college without a qualm and didn't go to pieces over my empty nest when they were all grown up.

"But ever since my son died, all I want is to have him back, even though my faith tells me he is in a better place. Will I ever be able to let go of him?"

No mortal being is ever truly ours to keep. I once came across an ancient Aztec prayer-poem that expresses this fact very well: "For such a little while you have loaned us to one another."

At the same time, there is a sense in which we never part from someone who has been dear to us, for those folks somehow weave themselves into our very being. We find ourselves echoing their mannerisms, their ideas, their enthusiasms. And we never have to let go of what has become so deeply a part of us, however much we may miss a person's physical presence. And so, in a very real sense, we carry that person with us wherever we go.

Reflect on these words that Saint Paul wrote many centuries ago about the power that binds you together: "Love never fails.... So faith, hope, love remain, these three; but the greatest of these is love" (1 Corinthians 13:8, 13, *New American Bible*).

Practice walking in that love—literally walking. As you make your way through the supermarket or the park or the office—wherever your feet carry you—remind yourself that you are carrying someone dear with your every step. Give thanks to the God who brought you together in love that the bond can never truly be broken.

Will I Recover My Sanity?

"I think I'm losing my mind," Marta told her best friend, Carrie. "I keep doing the darnedest things! Just the other day I went to put flowers on Jack's grave, and just as I bent down with them, I had an overpowering urge to turn around and run. And I did. I ran so far that I got myself good and lost! It took me half an hour or so to find my way back to my car.

"Another day I was in a clothing store and I stopped before a rack of red dresses. I've never worn red; it just doesn't look good on me. But it was Jack's favorite color. So I whipped out my credit card and came home with three. Isn't that crazy?"

"Maybe not," Carrie wisely replied. "I think you're just acting out your wish that Jack hadn't died. I suppose everyone goes through the same thing. I suppose that's why they say it's not wise to make life-changing decisions right after someone has died."

You, too, may feel that you are losing your mind. It is an altogether normal feeling. Writing about her own grief, one woman referred to a period she called "the crazies" when her actions seemed even to her to be quite out of control.

In Jesus' day, people who acted irrationally were often thought to be possessed by demons, and in a sense so are you. The demon whose name is grief has clouded your mind. Jesus often brought healing and peace of mind to such folks. Luke's Gospel tells of one such incident when Jesus drove a crowd of demons out of a man and sent them into a herd of pigs. Reflect on the outcome as Luke tells it: "Then people came out to see what had happened, and when they came to Jesus, they found the man from whom the demons had gone sitting at the feet of Jesus, clothed and in his right mind" (Luke 8:35).

In your prayer, entreat Jesus to free your mind and make you feel whole again. By his power, your demon will surely leave you, and your mind will be your own again. Some miraculous cures take a bit more time, but the healing power Jesus displayed in Israel is still in his possession. Express your trust to him.